277 Secrets Your Cat Wants You to Know

A Cat-alog of Unusual and Useful Information

Paulette Cooper
and
Paul Noble

Illustrated by Jack Fleming

TEN SPEED PRESS
BERKELEY, CALIFORNIA

Dedicated to Pinki and Pucci

1👁
Ten Speed Press
P.O. Box 7123
Berkeley, CA 94707

Distributed in Canada by Ten Speed Press Canada.

Cover photo by Image Bank

Text design by Nadja Lazansky

Illustrations by Jack Fleming

Printed in Canada

Library of Congress Cataloguing-in-Publication Data on file with publisher

ISBN 0-89815-952-0

5 6 7 8 — 02 01 00

Contents

Introduction

What you are about to read is the most informative, unusual—and quirky—book ever written on the subject of cats. It contains a "cat-alog" of interesting secrets, tips, findings, ideas, suggestions, and thoughts—all in an easy-to-read format—and is based mostly on the experience of cat owners and knowledgeable cat experts.

From them, you will learn how your cat can live a longer, healthier, and safer life; how you can be happier with your cat and vice versa; how to understand what your cat is trying to tell you so you can better communicate with him and comprehend what he is doing—and why; how to teach your cat a few simple things so he behaves better; and much, much more.

Just as we continually hear from people who have read our dog book, *277 Secrets Your Dog Wants You to Know*, telling us that it's the best dog book they've ever read, we hope to get similar feedback from cat lovers.

We do, however, apologize if the alternation of "he" and "she" in describing cats seems awkward. The cats we've "owned" (another term we apologize for) have been both male and female, but that's not why we chose to alternate pronouns. We just didn't want to leave either sex out by referring to our feline friends throughout as "he" or "she."

The following "pet-pourri" of interesting information is based on interviews, books, newspapers, newsletters, journal articles, and Internet newsgroup postings. Indeed, this is the first cat book to disseminate the experience of cat owners on the Internet to non-online cat people.

We wish to thank all those whose information and experiences we included (most of whom are named in the book), along with those on the "Cat Council." This was a group of our (mostly online) cat-owning friends who gave us their own cat secrets, tips, suggestions, and advice for this manuscript.

We promised to mention their cats. Alphabetically, so their cats won't be insulted, we thank the owners of: Cali (Gidaly); Calvin (Baker); Caviar and Truffle (Krinsky); Junior (Thomson); Katie (Friedman); Killer (Fleming); Leon and Dagny (Pignotti); Maxwell (Fendelman); Mr. Mojo Cat (Asherman); Quilty (Webb); Red "Fuzzlenuts" (Mayett); and Sweet Pea and Anthony (Pachtman).

We also wish to thank our talented and hardworking illustrator, Jack Fleming, for all the nights and weekends he gave up drawing all the wonderful pictures throughout.

We are most grateful to our veterinarian consultant, Dr. Mike Richards, an extraordinarily knowledgeable vet, who read through portions of this manuscript and helped us with the medical questions.

And where would we be without Albert Podell? (Indeed, since he introduced us!) As busy as this top matrimonial lawyer is, he took the time out to advise us and help us with our last three books.

Over at Ten Speed, we thank Clancy Drake for her excellent editing skills, cheerful personality, and for being such a pleasure to work with. Finally, there's Phil Wood and Jo Ann Deck at Ten Speed Press, who are not only great people but also terrific folks to work with, as we learned when we did our last book with them, *277 Secrets Your Dog Wants You To Know*.

Paulette Cooper & Paul Noble
PauletteC@aol.com
PaulRNoble@aol.com
or Paul & Paulette,
PO Box 20541, Cherokee Station,
NYC 10021

1. Nobody Ever Tells You These Things!

Is Alcohol Bad for Your Cat—and Is Yours Secretly Swilling Some on the Side?

You know your cat has a drinking problem when he won't drink out of his water bowl unless there's an olive in it! Actually, most cats don't like martinis, but some do like beer. "We've had cats whose owners tell us they're beer scavengers," said Dr. Mike Richards of Cobbs Creek, Virginia. "We even got a Scotch scavenger once—a high-class cat," he chuckled.

What would turn an ordinary housecat into a party animal? "I assume part of it is the yeasty taste that attracts them," said Richards, co-owner of Mathews Veterinary Services.

And some cats *really* develop a taste for it. Like Trixi, who belonged to pub owners in Wales. They couldn't figure out what was wrong with her—her vet even treated her for flu—until they discovered that she had acquired such a liking for beer, that she spent most of her time beneath the pub's drip trays behind the

---

HOW TO TELL IF YOUR CAT IS HUNG OVER

You may not know if your cat tied one on the night before. Pranksters, college kids, and neighbors who dislike cats may slip some alcohol to yours, and later you may be unaware what made him so sick.

To tell if your cat was drunk as a skunk (actually, drunk as a cat), watch out for these symptoms, says Louis Vine, D.V.M.

- Bleary eyes
- Listlessness
- Zapped-out looking
- Staggering
- A cat acting like a person with a bad headache

---

bar. After her owners found her staggering around the pub, they had to send her to a vet for two days to dry out!

Beer swilling among cats may be so prevalent—although rarely discussed—that for many years there's been a law on the books in Natchez, Mississippi, forbidding cats from drinking beer! And even today, at veterinary conferences, Dr. Louis Vine of South

---

IS MARIJUANA BAD FOR YOUR CAT?

The marijuana plant is related to catnip, so, in theory, it shouldn't be damaging to cats. But, in fact, it can make them hallucinate, possibly have seizures—and even die.

Marijuana is not as bad for a cat *psychologically* as it is for a dog. When dogs are given marijuana, sometimes blown in their face by stoned owners, they have no idea what's going on. They may become extremely confused and agitated since they don't have experience with something like catnip.

But just because something isn't as bad for a cat as it is for a dog doesn't mean it's good for a cat. So if Fluffy wants to share someone's joint with them, just say "no."

Carolina says doctors often bring up the subject of the "increase in alcoholic cats."

Although cats like yeast, some of the attraction may have little to do with that. "There's evidence that some animals have the urge to be intoxicated. Humans are not the only ones," Dr. Richards told us.

"I always thought if animals had access to alcohol, there would be a lot more problems than there are," he said. Still, you don't find many cats going to the Betty Ford Clinic for treatment—although they might need it. Felines are not good at metabolizing alcohol and even a moderate dose may start a cat vomiting; more could cause them to collapse or go into a coma.

So if your cat starts begging for some beer, tell him he's acting like a mad catter and that the bar is closed.

Should You Quit Smoking for Your Cat's Sake?

Quitting smoking would probably be a good idea for both of you. The only studies done on smokers' pets were on dogs, who turned out to be at greater risk for developing lung cancer than dogs whose owners were nonsmokers. This increased in dogs with short- and medium-length noses, probably because they lacked the efficient air filter of a long-nosed dog.

Since cats have short noses, they might face similar dangers, akin to someone living in a nightclub twenty-four hours a day, with never a chance to breathe fresh air.

Furthermore, cats face additional risks. Curiosity really could kill them, since some are fascinated by smoldering cigarettes in ashtrays and can burn themselves—or burn your house down— investigating them. Even unsmoked cigarettes lying around can pose a serious threat to cats, for if your cat ingests them, the tobacco can cause nicotine poisoning.

There's also a potential allergy problem. Cats are prone to allergies, and some are allergic to smoke.

And here's another danger. If you use transdermal nicotine patches, they're a potentially toxic threat to young children and pets. Even used patches contain enough medicine to cause acute poisoning in a small creature. Dispose of them carefully.

So you might hurt your cat if you smoke—and also if you quit. As they say, some days you just can't win. But if you smoke, you'll probably lose more.

Easy Ways to Toilet-Train Your Cat

Paul Kunkel, in his book *How to Toilet-Train Your Cat: 21 Days to a Litter-Free Home,* assures us that most cats *can* be trained to balance, squat on their hind legs, and expel into the toilet. But first, they have to be neutered, litter-trained, and able to jump to the toilet seat.

If your cat passes those hurdles, bring the litter box into the bathroom. Then, keep raising the litter box slowly to the level of the toilet seat, a few inches a day. Finally, on the big day (drum roll), move the litter box level with the top of the toilet.

Now here comes the weird part.

Remove the litter box altogether, and cover the toilet *under* the seat with strong plastic wrap, filled in the middle with your cat's litter. (During the training period, you will, of course, have to remove the plastic each time *you* want to use the facilities—and replace it when you're done.) Then, each day, decrease the amount of litter until he is peeing only into the plastic. When he's mastered that, make a hole in the middle of the plastic. And then, finally, you eliminate the plastic. It's as simple as that.

Well, maybe not. So you might find it helpful to buy the plastic toilet-training devices that are sold at major pet stores like Petland, Petsmart, Petco, etc. One type has herbs in it that you first

---

CAN CATS BE TAUGHT TO FLUSH THE TOILET?

Most can't. Flushing a toilet doesn't use any of your cat's standard paw or body movements and requires more lever pressure than most cats are capable of applying.

However, a few cats have supposedly been able to do it. Newspapers once reported the story of a cat owner receiving a $200-plus water bill for one month before realizing that his bored cat was flushing the toilet again and again while he was away during the day.

put in your cat's regular litter tray. Then you put the herbs in the toilet water to get your cat to associate the two.

If you have a toilet-trained cat, just remember always to leave the toilet seat down and the lid up! Otherwise, it doesn't matter how well your cat is toilet-trained—you'll have a mess: he'll never be able to lift that lid. But if the toilet seat is up, you're going to have a very wet cat.

CAN YOU CATCH SOMETHING FROM A TOILET SEAT USED BY YOUR CAT?

Whenever a cat goes outdoors, or spends time with infected animals (or humans), he can catch fleas, parasites, or ringworm. Since transmission is generally via the cat's fur and not his paws, and since it's the paws that a toilet-trained cat would place on the toilet seat, the likelihood of your catching something from sharing a toilet seat is probably equal to being struck by lightning at the moment you win a million-dollar lottery.

Should Your Cat Go on Prozac?

It's the designer drug of the '90s for people, so shouldn't your cat be part of the Prozac Nation, too? "I give cats Prozac for a number of reasons," says top veterinary dermatologist/behaviorist, Dr. Steven Melman, who is sometimes jocularly called "The Pied Piper of Prozac for Pets."

Dr. Melman, of the Animal Dermatology/Behavior Clinic in Potomac, Maryland, told us that cats are most often given Prozac for "obsessive-compulsive disorders, like when they pull their hair out for non-allergy reasons."

This psychological problem corresponds to obsessive-compulsive disorder in people. But it can be more harmful, since a compulsive cat can't check the door five times to see if it's locked when he goes out, or make sure not to step on a crack when walking down the street.

But Prozac (fluoxetine) has been known to help with this problem, as well as with possibly related nipple, flank, and feet sucking. Prozac also works for certain types of aggression, and for Situational Adjustment Disorder or SAD. "Cats become upset for various reasons: say their families are breaking up, or their owner has a new boyfriend or girlfriend, or is moving," says Melman.

Of course a cat can't directly tell you he's upset over these things, but the most common manifestation of distress is "inappropriate urination and defecation, or howling. And Prozac may help with all of these," Dr. Melman stated.

Incidentally, if your cat is displaying these symptoms, and you're on Prozac, don't give your cat your medicine; the dosages are different. And, for the same reason, don't take your cat's pill if you're having a Prozac moment.

Should You Vacuum Your Cat?

Vacuuming your cat is a great way to get rid of dry skin flakes, dander, loose shedding hair, flea dirt, and, especially, fleas themselves.

The only trouble: very few cats enjoy it.

Oh, there's the occasional cat who likes to be vacuumed, and whose owner took a picture of it happening and posted it on the Internet to prove it. And there are people who swear their cats love to have certain parts of their bodies, like their heads, vacuumed. (That's vacuumed, not examined.) But when most cats hear the sound of a vacuum, they're out of there.

Enter a special hand-held, lightweight, battery-operated vacuum called Pet Vac II. Since it grabs hair before it becomes airborne—unlike hand brushing, which sends dander and fur flying in the air—Pet Vac can be a lifesaver for people—and cats—with allergies.

A convincing argument can be made for the benefits of vacuuming your cat, but you'll have to convince him of it as well. Apparently, the developer of the Pet Vac II, Jim Wessling, has only been partially successful. "We have two cats," he told us. "One of them loves it when I vacuum him. The other my wife has to do."

Everything Your Cat Wants to Know About Catnip But Is Too High to Ask

IS IT LIKE A DRUG? Catnip contains a hallucinogenic compound, and the *American Journal of Veterinary Research* reported in 1972 that the chemical structure of the active ingredient in catnip is similar to LSD.

It's been said that the oil does for some cats what marijuana does for some people. So, okay, your cat *is* tripping on it. But since it won't fry his brain, and he isn't going to raid your refrigerator and eat all your ice cream, or rob you to get money to buy more catnip, why worry?

IS IT LIKE SEX? Yes, it makes cats as happy as having sex does, affecting them the same way as natural sex pheromones do by stimulating the same centers in the brain.

But since your cat's playing with catnip won't leave you with a houseful of kittens you can't get anyone to adopt, you're probably better off finding some catnip for him than another cat to "play" with.

WHAT IS CATNIP ANYWAY? There are over 250 varieties of catnip or *Nepeta cataria,* and it's easy to grow. If you smell it, you'll see that it's part of the mint family. Catnip is also related to valerian

---

WILL CATNIP MAKE YOU HIGH?

Back in the '60s it was big news when it was revealed that catnip produced a "marijuana-like intoxication." Even one of America's most prestigious medical journals printed a photo showing the leaves of the catnip plant, to prove how much they resembled those of a marijuana plant.

Well, it looked like a marijuana plant because it was one. Somebody made a mistake, and it turned out that the herb they tested and pictured was, in fact, marijuana.

(Valeriana officinalis), which causes a similar reaction in cats, but smells terrible to them. No doubt that's why you never see pet shops selling valerian-stuffed toys.

HOW SENSITIVE IS A CAT TO CATNIP? It's been said that cats can smell as little as one part per billion in the air.

DOES IT AFFECT A CAT PHYSICALLY AS WELL AS PSYCHOLOGICALLY? Yes, it does cause his little heart to beat faster. But so do running and most other rigorous or pleasurable activities, so don't let that worry you. By the way, when catnip is given to cats internally, it actually acts as a tranquilizer and slows them down.

IF A CAT DOESN'T LIKE CATNIP, IS THERE SOMETHING WRONG WITH HIM? Not all cats like it, and no cats like it early in their lives. Although it appears to be genetically determined whether a cat is attracted to it, two kittens from the same litter may not have the same reaction to catnip.

WHO DISCOVERED CATS LIKE IT? It was probably first used on lions, after circus trainers somehow discovered that it made them more docile.

DO CATS EVER GET "BUMMED OUT" FROM IT? Yes, cats have been known to have a "bad trip." They don't get paranoid and think mice are chasing them, but they do occasionally become extremely agitated.

As to whether it's addictive, experts disagree. Most say no, but one of the most famous animal researchers in the world, Dr. Michael Fox, wrote that cats *can* become addicted to it, even leaving their food for it.

If you see this happening, stop giving him his catnip fix. It's probably a good idea in general not to give cats *too* much catnip, or to leave it out all the time.

WHAT'S THE BEST WAY TO HANDLE IT/CHOOSE IT/BUY IT? Catnip is very perishable, so you should handle it gently.

• To tell if it's fresh, take some between your fingers, squeeze it, and sniff it.

- Always keep it in a sealed container in the refrigerator.
- Since the scent does fade, freshen a catnip toy frequently with a fresh dose of it.

Should You Use Catnip, Too?

Although catnip stimulates cats, it relaxes people, and the plant has been used by people for thousands of years. The two ways it's commonly used are:

- **Catnip tea:** If you want to try this, don't boil the leaves; this drives all the healing oils out of them into the air. Pour very hot—but not boiling—water over the leaves, and let them sit for ten to fifteen minutes. You can add one-third teaspoon of powdered ginger or 1 teaspoon of grated ginger.

- **For cuts and wounds:** Studies show catnip has a natural healing quality. Take a fresh plant and tear off several leaves, crush them, wet them a bit, and apply them to a cut.

Don't Be Shocked When Petting Your Cat

Here are some things that may reduce static charge, that electrifying experience of touching something and going *aaagh...*

- Increase the water content of the air with a humidifier, a teakettle, or even a hot shower with the bathroom door open.
- Test your shoes to see if some pairs generate less static on the carpet than others, suggests *Catnip* newsletter, published at Tufts University School of Veterinary Medicine.
- Pet your cat in the bath or kitchen where there is no carpet and the moisture is higher.
- Bathe your cat with a shampoo and conditioner.
- Run a fabric softener sheet backward over your cat's fur. (You may not want to do this, as fabric softeners contain chemicals.)
- The *New York Times,* in its Science Times Q&A column, said to touch a water pipe, faucet, or other grounding device before touching your cat. To prevent a strong shock to yourself, touch the keys from your pocket to the pipe.

Even better, they suggested you buy an antistatic spray, which prevents static cling in clothes, and spray it on your clothes and carpet—not on your cat.

2. Embarrassing Behavior of Your Cat—Including Sex— You've Been Ashamed to Ask Anyone About

Poop Problems

MY CAT HAS BEEN STRAINING TO MOVE HIS BOWELS. SHOULD I USE ONE OF THE PREPACKAGED PET ENEMAS? No. *CATsumer Report* newsletter says these may contain high concentrations of phosphates, which could cause a calcium imbalance and lead to serious problems. Try adding fiber to your cat's diet instead.

---

5 WAYS TO STOP STINKY LITTER BOXES

- Try a new type of food, especially a better one, like a premium cat food.
- Buy a commercial product like *Primera*, that you spray on their food. Such products help reduce the smell of feces and urine.
- Try recycled-newspaper kitty litter, or litter made of wheat or alfalfa pellets, which may reduce the odor.
- Keep the box clean.
- Get rid of liners, since they wrinkle, causing them to catch and hold the waste.

MY CAT KEEPS PASSING GAS. WHAT SHOULD I DO? Leave the room. Seriously, this can be a big problem, especially with older cats, whose digestion may become sluggish.

A natural remedy is a small amount of low-fat yogurt or half a capsule of acidophilus mixed in with each meal. You can also buy

CurTail, produced by the same company that makes *Beano,* which reduces gas in people. *CurTail* reportedly does the same for cats and dogs. Or just try changing his food.

MY CAT LIKES TO PLAY "POOP HOCKEY" AND KNOCK HIS STOOL OUT OF HIS BOX. Give him a Ping-Pong ball to play with instead. Or get a deeper litter box with a rim. Or a hooded one so he can't knock anything out.

You can also mitigate the problem by cleaning the litter box frequently, scooping up the solids as soon as they appear.

MY CAT LIKES TO EAT THE STUFF (ECCCCHHH). This is disgusting to us, but natural to animals. Newborn kittens can't urinate or defecate until their mothers lick their tummies and bottoms. Their mothers also clean up their waste products for them, and since they don't know to use mops and sponges ... It might help to give your cat more fiber. Some suggest putting something unpleasant on the waste itself, like Tabasco sauce.

MY CAT SOMETIMES LEAVES HIS FECES IN VARIOUS PLACES ABOUT THE HOUSE. Famed animal behaviorist Desmond Morris says, in *Catwatching,* that cats may not always feel compelled to cover their droppings because they may want to advertise that they are the dominant cat. By deliberately displaying their feces at strategic points, they assert their authority and show that they're in charge, especially if there are other cats in the house.

If your cat does this, standard litter box retraining techniques may help. For example, getting additional litter boxes, changing them more frequently, etc.

WHEN I GO AWAY, MY CAT POOPS ON MY CLOTHES. He isn't doing it out of spite. Just as he follows scents to get home, he may be doing it to help you find your way back to the house.

Rear End Problems

I've got a butt-dragging cat who keeps biting at his rear. There could be dried feces, worms, matted hair, or even a stuck blade of grass back there. But the most common cause is impacted anal sacs.

Put a little Vaseline or baby oil on the anus to soothe the irritation. If it happens more than once, take your cat to the vet, and give him the unpleasant job of emptying these sacs. A high-fiber diet may help prevent this in the future, making your cat and your vet very happy.

My cat has some disgusting yellow stuff that comes from his hindquarters. These anal secretions are not uncommon—especially when a cat is nervous or upset. If it happens frequently, see a vet.

My cats sniff other cats' derrieres. Cats have scent glands under their tails on either side of the anus, so they're just checking each other out. The dominant cat is the one who sniffs first, but cat hierarchies aren't rigid. The top cat today could be the bottom one tomorrow; the sniffer may become the sniffee.

I have a long-haired cat who occasionally gets stool (or urine) stuck on her fur in the back. Wash the area with a damp washcloth and then rub a little cornstarch into the hair to get rid of the smell. Try a change in diet, and if that doesn't help, you may want to keep the hair cut back there so that you're not forever holding your nose and cleaning him.

Urine Problems

MY CAT LIKES TO SMELL OTHER CATS' URINE. This is perfectly natural and not at all disgusting to them. Smelling it may tell them such things as the sex of the other cat and whether it's sexually receptive or lives nearby.

MY CAT PUTS HIS HEAD IN HIS OWN URINE. When a cat sprays after running into another cat, he will generally rub his cheeks in his sprayed urine. Remember that sex glands on a cat's face are involved in sexual attraction.

IF YOUR CAT'S BREATH TAKES YOURS AWAY

If your cat's breath could knock the Statue of Liberty off her perch, there are a few things you can do. Some remedies that work for humans may help your cat too. Remember that old rhyme, "If you will eat a piece of parsley, you needn't eat your onions sparsely"? The same is true for your cat, except that she shouldn't have onions—but a little parsley's fine and may help. There are also some commercially available mouthwashes for cats.

Still, rather than masking the smell, you may want to find out what is causing it. If it smells like bad urine is coming from your cat's mouth, she may have gum problems (like recession), tooth problems, or mouth infections. So stop holding your breath when you get near hers, and take her to a vet.

Sex Problems

My cat sneers when he sees a cat of the opposite sex. That look of "contempt" is actually "flehming." The cat takes an odor and intensifies it by sending it up to another sense organ in his head. Almost all male cats flehm when they investigate the genitals of a female cat, and some female cats do it also.

When I pet my cat near her tail, it immediately shoots up. Although it's been jokingly referred to as "tail erection," cats do this because when they were kittens and their mothers cleaned them, they raised their tails so she could "inspect" the area.

MALES BEHAVING BADLY

The male cat's sex organ makes its first public appearance when the soon-to-be studmuffin is only a couple of weeks old and a slight bulge appears beneath the tail. Some cats are able to produce sperm when they're only 5 months old, which would be the equivalent of that happening in a boy around $7^1/_2$ years old.

From the time the male cat reaches sexual maturity, unless he's altered, his sex drive will not only lead his life, but may lead to his death. It's what causes him to roam the streets where he may get hit by cars, or poisoned or injured, or encounter other obstacles that may kill him or prevent him from ever making it back to his house. His sex drive also causes him to get into fights, mostly with other males who dare to enter what he considers to be his territory. These fights can lead to severe injuries, and occasionally death.

Although a male cat will do anything to get to a female in heat—he may pursue one female for days—once he finds her, it's hardly the cat's meow for her. Among cats, there's no human-like concept of "pleasuring." Mating lasts a few seconds, slam-bam-without-even-a-thank-you-ma'am, with no foreplay, afterplay, smooching, cuddling, cocktails before, or cigarette afterwards.

IS YOUR CAT KINKY?

- Cats masturbate, and that little shudder afterwards doesn't mean they're cold. They can have tiny "orgasms" as well.
- A sexually aroused cat may come on to a dog.
- A male cat may impregnate his own sister and attempt sex with his own kittens.
- Cats may be aroused by their owner's arms, armpits, heads, and breasts; soft pillows; fuzzy slippers; smelly clothes, etc.
- Cats may act seductively toward their owners during their fertile period. They'll rub their chins and faces on them, raise their rears, become extremely affectionate, and lick and display themselves.

WHEN MY MALE CAT SEES A FEMALE ONE, HIS JAWS START CHATTERING LECHEROUSLY. Cats sometimes also do this in anticipation of eating something delicious, like when they see potential prey, such as a bird.

MY CATS MOUNT EACH OTHER. They may be displaying sexual interest, or it may be a sign of dominance—or even just plain old boredom. That's probably sometimes true for people, too!

What to Expect When Your Cat Is Expecting

Here are some things to expect if your cat is pregnant, told to us by Steve Aiken, an animal behaviorist from Wichita, Kansas.

Expect kittens if your female cat's been fooling around: Cats are much better at reproduction than humans, and if they've been having some fun, they will probably have something small and furry around soon to show for it.

Kitty Kondoms

Little latex condoms to put on your pet's peter? Are these for real? Actually not, but they are an interesting gift. Just remind the recipients that if they want to try and put the Kitty Kondoms on their cat, they should wear *very* heavy gloves.

Seriously, they shouldn't put them on their cat, and the kondoms don't work, but spaying and neutering your cat does. Reminding people to fix their cats is the purpose of this product, and each $2.95 package of "rubbers" also contains a pep talk (written by KK's developer, author and radio commentator John Stewart) about neutering and spaying your cat.

Still, Kitty Kondoms is a cute gag gift. "Give a package to a first-time owner while maintaining a very straight face," suggests Stewart.

Expect the kittens to arrive in about two months: Pregnancy lasts 57–70 days. It takes about three weeks after conception before there are signs that the mother is pregnant, but you won't be able to feel the kittens moving until the last few weeks.

Expect that sometimes your female cat may be "faking it": Some female cats go through false pregnancies, even developing false labor. They produce milk, and occasionally go into a depressed state after the "false whelping" when there are no kittens to care for.

Expect that the kittens won't all arrive at once: Cats may deliver one or more kittens after the main litter, sometimes even a day later.

Expect newborn kittens to be "sensitive": Their sense of smell is so well developed at birth that they can find their mothers' nipples by smell (and heat) alone.

Expect the kittens' father to be blasé at best: Some fathers are solicitous of the mother cat. But others couldn't care less. Many don't even recognize the kittens as theirs—which is perhaps understandable since some of the kittens may not be. Female cats can be impregnated by more than one male, and cats in a litter may have more than one father.

Expect something new every day: The kittens' eyes will begin to open when they're 5 to 10 days old. They'll be fully open at about 20 days, and by then, the kittens will have begun to crawl.

A week later, they'll be wrestling with the other kittens. By 3 to 4 weeks, they'll be eating solid foods and learning to use the litter box. At 5 to 6 weeks, they're ready to begin weaning. And soon, your female may be pregnant again.

Expect to spay your cat: Think about neutering her so you don't have to find homes for the next litter.

ARE FEMALE CATS NYMPHOMANIACS?

The female may start slower, but she's usually the one with the most sexual stamina. After she has copulated with the male cat a few times, if her totally exhausted mate wants to stop, tough. She may push him to do another round—or even six.

Some females will wait until the male is ready to start again, while others don't pussyfoot around. If her man isn't interested in another roll in the hay, the lady may just go and find someone else to service her. Indeed, she may mate up to 15 times per session with a half dozen different males during one cycle, and sex can go on for hours—even days.

The Big Fix: Bad Reasons Not to Neuter Your Cat

- **You'll be less macho:** Men, especially, sometimes feel that it reflects on their masculinity if their cats are altered. Mike Capuzzo, in *Wild Things,* quotes a female veterinarian as saying that fixing your pet will not "prevent you from buying a red sports car and growing your hair extra long on one side to hide the thin part."

- **It costs money:** So do kittens, but there are low-cost spaying programs available.

- **You want adorable kittens around and you're sure you'll be able to give them away later:** It's not so easy to give away kittens, especially after you've imposed on your friends for the first litter.

- **Your cat will get fat:** Your cat will get fat from too much eating and too little exercising, not from getting neutered.

- **Your cat will get lazy:** Is it better for them to be active and miserable because they are sexually frustrated?

- **It's cruel to take away an animal's sexuality:** It's cruel to an owner to live with a spraying cat, or the howling of a sexually frustrated female in heat.

- **Reducing their sex drive takes away a lot of your cat's fun:** It also denies your cat a lot of problems and dangers, along with a shorter life.

10 Simple Ways to Stop Your Cat from Spraying

Male cats cause the most problems by spraying. Female cats also spray, but not as frequently, and it doesn't smell as bad. It's the males who have the—shall we say—piquant odors. To diminish this problem:

Neuter your cat before he starts spraying: Sometimes he will spray afterwards, depending on how ingrained the habit was and how successful the surgery was. Since the more a cat sprays the more he will spray, neuter him early.

Alternately, neuter your cat the minute he starts spraying: Even if the surgery is successful, he will probably continue to spray for a short while.

Get rid of the smell so far: The less your cat smells of it, the less he'll repeat doing it, so wash the area—including the walls— with a commercial-strength cleaner. If he's sprayed on a carpet, you may have to clean the pad also if it's soaked through.

HOW TO TELL IF HE'S URINATING OR SPRAYING

A cat's probably spraying when he backs up to walls and twitches his tail or treads his hind feet, or sniffs the area before (not after) marking it, or only releases a small amount of liquid.

Urinating is usually done in a squatting position, on a horizontal surface, and the cat makes scratching motions afterwards.

Block where he sprays with food and water: Cats usually spray in one place, so put food or water dishes there, which may discourage him since cats don't like to spray where they eat.

Put aluminum foil over the spot: This may keep him from returning to the place, partially because cats don't like their feet to get wet, and if they urinate where the foil is, it will hold the spray so they'll be standing in it.

Reduce his exposure to other cats: More than one cat in your house—especially a female in heat—often increases your cat's spraying. If you were thinking of getting another cat, think again, or introduce the new cat into your house very slowly.

Reduce the area he defends: A cat is defending his territory by spraying, so give him less to "patrol" by making larger areas inaccessible to him. For example, if you live in a three-story house and he's spraying all over the place, put a gate up so he can't go above the first floor.

Block your cat's view: Cats may spray when they look out the window and see other cats, so try to cover the vista.

Reduce the chaos: Cats most likely to spray even after surgery are those in chaotic homes containing children, other pets, and no regular schedule.

Put kitty diapers on your cat: Honest. These work.

NEW PRODUCT TO END CAT SPRAYING

A product has recently been developed by a veterinary specialist in Europe who discovered that cats do not spray on objects previously marked with facial pheromones. Within 10 days of applying this product, called Feliway, there's supposedly an 80 percent reduction in your cat's spraying. While the product is only available in Europe now, it is expected to come to the United States soon.

Cornell University College of Veterinary Medicine's *Animal Health Newsletter* reported good results in America using buspirone, an anxiety drug that reduced spraying by 75 percent. Many veterinarians are also prescribing Elavil for this problem.

Stopping a Stray or Neighboring Cat from Spraying Near Your Home

Since the scent may make your cat spray more, you should check carefully to see if another cat has sprayed, especially near doors and windows. Here are a few ways to discourage him from coming back:

Neutering your own female takes away the attraction.

Pour vinegar on the offending cat's spray: This helps to eliminate or cover the odor, so the cat is less likely to return, and your cat is therefore less likely to spray in response. You can also use cotton balls soaked in nail polish remover.

Mark your territory: John Avalon Reed's *The Whole Kitty Catalog*, which is filled with blurbs of terrific products and interesting ideas, suggested that you take some feces out of your cat's box and mark the outside territory of your yard, since some cats won't cross over that. The idea probably works, but do you really want your house ringed with that?

A (probably) less effective but more refined method is to sprinkle orange and lemon rinds around the outside of your house.

STOPPING A CAT IN THE MIDDLE OF A SPRAY

You know by now that the less your cat sprays, the less likely he is to spray in the future. So if you catch your cat in the act, try to stop him on the spot. Don't yell at him and make a big deal out of it. That just increases his arousal and could make his desire to spray even harder to control, says behaviorist Dr. John Wright, author of the best-seller *Is Your Cat Crazy?* Instead, he suggests two other ways of stopping your cat in mid-stream.

- **Touch his tail:** Just put it down when he raises it. This inhibits the spraying.

- **Call his name:** If you see him starting to back up and quiver his tail, calmly interrupt the behavior.

3. Getting Your Cat to Love You More

15 Ways Your Cat Shows How He Likes You

It may be very apparent when your little fur baby says, "I hate you," but most cats are not as obvious when they say "I like you." But they do say it, and our inability to understand it may be one reason cats have a reputation for being unfriendly and unloving.

Yet cats do show affection, not only toward people but to other cats, sometimes even by helping them give birth and care for their kittens.

You can see many other signs of affection among cats. They may rub their bodies under each other's chins, or groom each other, or lightly brush against each other, transferring scents, sort of expressing a feline version of a "high five" to the other cat. How do they express their affection for you?

- The best known way a cat shows he cares is to wrap his tail around you, bump his head or body against you or your legs, or rub the back of his ears or his face on you. This is to give you a familiar odor, make him feel more comfortable with you, or claim you as his territory.
- He may lick you, which is similar to the grooming one cat does to another to show trust and affection.
- He may lick himself after we pet him or rub against him (rubbing our own scent on him), "tasting" our scent. We can't always smell the odor from our hands, but cats can.
- When a cat curls on your lap, it is a sure sign of affection. Okay, your lap's probably the warmest spot around, but he isn't going to be on someone he doesn't like.
- Sucking or licking your skin or clothes may be aimed more at you than at something you're wearing, or something you have on you that they like.

- Kneading you may mean a cat sees you as his mother; cats don't knead people they don't need. (Sorry about that.)
- Drooling is something many cats do when they're extremely happy or while kneading someone. It is more common among cats who were weaned too early and can be a sign of regression to kittenhood. It can also be a sign of physical problems, though, so watch your cat carefully if he suddenly starts drooling.
- Bringing you a present, like a dead mouse or a bird, is a reflection of his affection and a reaffirmation that you're his mommy.
- If a cat holds his tail in a vertical position, it is a very strong sign of affection. In fact, you'll notice that when your cat approaches a person or other cat that he doesn't know, he keeps his tail down until he's sure that he is safe.
- Rolling over to one side means "play with me." Cats don't want to play with people they don't like.
- Resting a paw on your arm is a gentle and reassuring gesture of affection.
- Stretching on you is another sign of affection, especially when he's planted his two front feet as high as he can on your leg.
- Some cats like to lick your eyelids to wake you in the morning.
- Arching his back softly and slowly, while rubbing against your legs is a cat's way of saying "I love you."
- Listen for a chirping sound. Cats purr for lots of reasons, but if your cat chirps while rubbing up against you, he's really thrilled with you.

10 Ways to Get Your Cat to Love You More

There was a company once that made an entire line of cosmetics, body lotions, and shampoos containing catnip to encourage cats to get close to those who used these products. They're no longer on the market—although one could make a homemade version with one's own catnip—but there are better ways to get your little love to be more of a lap cat. After all, you want your cat to come to you and love you for yourself, not for your catnip. Here are some catnip-free ways to strengthen that animal-owner bond:

1. If your cat doesn't want to let you touch her, buy a toy you two can play with together that keeps her near you without any direct physical contact. For example, a toy attached to a string. Then, keep shortening the string so your cat becomes increasingly more comfortable as she is closer to you.

2. At Tufts University School of Veterinary Medicine, they suggest that if a cat will generally spend one minute on your lap before bolting, after about thirty seconds, offer her a small food reward. Then, each time she sits in your lap, extend the period a few seconds, reinforcing her at forty, fifty, sixty seconds, and so on. Eventually she may sit still for a while on your lap without having to be constantly reinforced.

3. Handle gently. Aloof, skittish cats may be mellowed by handling. Cuddle your cat whenever she lets you.

4. Be low-key. Don't make fast moves. Minimize loud sounds.

5. Don't be pushy. Let her come to you when she's ready, rather than your coming to her when you are. "Don't love your cat when *you* want to. Take your cue from her. She'll be more attentive to you if the attention is not forced," says Dr. Margaret Muns, staff veterinarian in the TW Dogs and Cats Forum at CompuServe.

6. Talk to her gently and softly as you put down her food, so she associates you with her favorite activity—eating. Stay in the area while she eats.

7. Massage her, if she likes it.

8. Ignore her. Some say *not* looking at your cat or having anything to do with her when you first get her—other than feeding her, of course—will lead the cat to come to you.

9. Spend as much time around her as possible—you can be reading or eating or whatever—so she gets used to being with you without feeling threatened.

10. Don't use negative reinforcement. Don't scold her and don't ever hit her. Punishment doesn't work, and with one loud scream or slap, you can undo all the other nine things above that were working so well for you.

P.S. Some human males also claim great success with women by following items 3–10.

---

3 TIPS FOR CHOOSING A LOVING "PEOPLE CAT"

Most people prefer a cuddly cat, and a few studies have been done in this area that might help you choose a more loving pet.

1. Kittens from large families generally grow up to be more loving cats.

2. The critical socialization period for kittens is between two and five weeks of age, at which time it's important that they have positive human interaction. Of course it isn't just those three weeks that matter. Kittens handled from birth develop into warmer, cuddlier, almost doglike creatures, while kittens lacking this human contact are more likely to become skittish and aloof.

3. Finally, the age of that kitty in the window is very important. Some pet stores put kittens out to sell at around seven to eight weeks because they're smaller and cuter then. But if you want what arrives on little cat's feet to grow up to be a friendly healthy cat, your kitten should remain with her mother until she's close to three months old.

Survey:

WHO GIVES YOU MORE AFFECTION: YOUR CAT OR YOUR SIGNIFICANT OTHER?

The significant others lost out in the affection department. First, the "more affection from the cats" side.

"I get licked more by the cat than the husband."

"My significant other visits, but my cat is always there."

"My cat loves me unconditionally, doesn't leave the toilet seat up, purrs when stroked, and shows appreciation for the things I do for her." (Kim Baker, South Africa)

"My cat's snits are usually brief—and he doesn't talk to me while I'm writing." (Shelley Thomson, California)

Some thought they got equal affection from the cat and their significant other:

"Both give affection and ignore me in exactly the same way." (Jack Fleming, Arizona)

"My husband gives me more affection in terms of quantity. But in terms of quality, when one of my cats decides to be affectionate with me, it is the highest-quality affection in the whole world and it makes me happy in a way that no human being ever could."

"It's a toss-up. I scratch my husband's back for twenty minutes each night and my cat is trying to weasel his way into the act so I have to scratch hubby, then cat, then hubby, then cat." (Joni Webb, Texas)

And votes for the significant other:

"My cat is rude, spoiled, nasty, and manipulative, a shoe-eating, hairball-hacking, purse-chewing, furniture-scratching, morning-howling orange tabby—and I get more affection from dead houseplants." (Leah Sherman, New York)

Is It Safe to Kiss Your Cat?

Many loving owners do occasionally plant a little kiss on their favorite furball, but is a kiss just a kiss, or is it a potential health hazard?

There's probably little to worry about germ-wise, according to Dr. James Miller of the Atlantic Veterinary College at the University of Prince Edward Island in Canada. "It's probably more dangerous to kiss a person than a cat," he told us. "You're more likely to get a viral disease from a human than from a feline."

This expert on zoonosis isn't saying you can't catch *anything.* "What you might get from kissing your cat is strep, if your cat is a carrier in the oral cavity. But it's highly unlikely."

On the other hand, if you get close enough to your cat's mouth to kiss near its snout or lips, the real danger is not in your cat transferring germs to you, but that your cat will react to the closeness by turning on you and biting you, which could lead to diseases.

Even without a bite though, your cat could give you cat scratch disease if it licks you. "Cat scratch disease doesn't only come from a scratch. It can happen if your cat licks you as well as bites you and you have a break in the skin," Dr. Miller stressed.

"Let's say you have a cut on your lip. If your cat licks you there, he could conceivably transmit cat scratch disease to you. But cats aren't big lip kissers, although they may lick open wounds, which could transmit the disease," he stated.

Should you kiss your cat then? If you're lucky enough to have a cat who's that affectionate, and if you care enough about this subject to even be reading this, you aren't going to stop because someone tells you to, so the heck with it. You might be hit by lightning if you go out during a storm, and you're not going to stay indoors. So kiss away.

How Your Cat Kisses You

If your cat actually kisses you, it's unusual, because few cats kiss in the traditional face-to-face manner of people. Dogs do, because they learned as puppies to lick their mothers' mouths to get food from them. But cats don't feed their offspring in that manner, so face-oriented licking, i.e., kissing, never developed for cats as it did for dogs. Thus, if your cat is not an active kisser or licker of humans, blame it on evolution, not his lack of love for you.

Remember too that cats don't usually smooch amongst themselves. Their affection is displayed by greeting each other with nose touches, grooming each other, playful biting, or rubbing up against each other. So don't be insulted that they don't act differently toward you.

But some people have cats that lick hands and faces like dogs do. Some cats even touch their noses or mouths right to their owners' lips, or lick their mouths with their tongues, or use their paws to hug their owners.

If you're lucky enough to get any kind of royal feline treatment (except for the biting), accept it as your cat's way of kissing you. If he licks you or rubs his nose or body against you, or marks you as his own by stroking and rubbing you, consider it a sign of love. "The more heavily you will be scented by your cat, the more beloved you will be," says Dr. Michael Fox.

One cat expert says the real exchange of kisses, feline style, is with the eyes and not the mouth anyway. When your little purr-baby half-closes his eyes, he's showing trust and confidence. So, if he looks at you and his eyelids close momentarily and then reopen to resume the gaze, "you've been kissed by your cat" says "Felicitude," the pen name for Daphne Negus, editor of *Cat World* magazine.

How to Get Your Cat to Like Someone He Hates

Do all guests have to be approved by your cat? Does he hate people in your family no matter how hard they try to gain his affection? Here are a few things your poor cat-despised friend can do.

First, have this person be the *only* one in your family to feed your cat. They should also try to remain in the room while your cat is eating—not too close or your cat may refuse the food, but near enough that your cat is aware of the presence but not turned off by it.

If your cat absolutely and positively won't eat while they're there, have them leave. But they should make sure at the very least that the cat saw who put the food down for him.

In addition to feeding, the rejected person should also try to

---

WHY CATS GO TO PEOPLE WHO HATE THEM

Ever notice how your cat sometimes goes toward the one person who doesn't like cats? That may be because that's the person who's not staring at him, thrusting their hands out, trying to get the cat to come to them. Since they're not attracted to cats, cat haters are the ones sitting still and looking elsewhere. Because your cat finds them the least threatening, he is attracted toward them.

If they want the cat to stay away from them, they should stare at him with wide-open eyes, moving their hands around a lot to try to convince the cat to come over to them. The cat will then most likely avoid them.

Another theory about why cats gravitate toward those who don't appreciate it, is that cats sense when they're rejected and want to get the upper paw. So the more someone avoids a cat, the more the cat insists on putting his scent on that person.

---

play with the cat from afar, maybe with a "long-distance toy" like one of those laser-beam toys or motorized mice.

They might also try putting something with their scent near the cat's bedding—for example, leaving their undershirt near where the cat sits.

Finally, they could change their scent and see if that alters the cat's attitude toward them. The cat's dislike of them could be caused by something like their toothpaste, which could have mint. Most cats do not like mint (which is odd, since catnip comes from the mint family).

How Your Cat Likes to Be Massaged, Scratched, Tickled, Touched, Rubbed, or Petted

You can go to a professional masseuse for your cat, but, of course, that costs money. "I bought a pet to calm me down, and now I have to pay $70 to relax the animal?" one person asked *Daily News* writer K. C. Baker.

You don't have to rub your cat the wrong way. Just use the techniques outlined by Jane Buckle, an expert on anatomy and physiology, and author of *How to Massage Your Cat.*

She suggests you start a massage session by finding a comfortable place for your cat—like your lap—away from breakable objects, in case your cat suddenly bolts.

Use gentle pressure at first until you know how much your cat is ready to accept. Then, here are some motions she recommends:

• Comb your cat's fur with two fingertips, up and down his body.
• Thumb the fur simultaneously on both sides of his spine.
• Draw circles with three fingers, using both hands, on his body, including his chest.
• Massage his tail, slowly, to its tip.

WHY DO SOME CATS LIKE TO BE PETTED?

Since mother cats groom their kittens, when we pet our cats they probably feel like their mothers are once again grooming them. They become kittens again, with Mummy taking care of them.

Many adult cats who like to be petted will approach their owners with their tails erect as a signal they want to be petted. They also did this as kittens when they wanted their mother's attention. And if you give it to them, just listen to that power purring!

Why Some Cats Attack When You Pet Them

The most common theory explaining why cats attack is that for them to allow humans to stroke them is unnatural. After all, cats are basically wild creatures, and under different circumstances we would be their enemies, not their masseurs or masseuses. Their instincts to protect themselves win out over their desire to enjoy themselves, and they attack.

Dr. Bonnie Beaver, a noted pet researcher, has a different theory. She says that cats become so comfortable when being stroked that they fall asleep. When they suddenly awaken, they become confused, uncertain what's happening.

What if we fell asleep and woke up to find ourselves on the lap of the Jolly Green Giant, being stroked? We'd say, "What the heck am I doing here?", lash out, and dash out, just like your cat does.

Ms. Buckle points out that cats especially like to be massaged and petted where they have the most glands, like under their chins, around their cheeks, and at the base of the tail. They also like to be rubbed where they can't reach, like the back of their ears.

But be very watchful that your cat doesn't suddenly turn on you. Learn to spot the signs; for some cats, massaging them is just rubbing them the wrong way.

What Your Cat Likes Best

Try these simple no-cost ways to make your cat happier, and she will repay you with more love and closeness.

TO HELP HER BE MORE OF A CAT:

- Get a birdhouse, birdbath, or bird feeder so she can watch the birds outside.
- Plant something that attracts butterflies and insects. If she's an indoor cat, put the plants near the window so she can watch the little visitors.
- Cats like height. Put a secure beam up, so the cat can leap up on it and then look down from this perch.
- Don't mow your lawn too close. Cats like to hide in the grass, stalking birds from where they can't be seen, and then rush forward at their prey. (But don't let your cat hurt the birds!)

TO MAKE YOUR CAT MORE CONTENTED AND COMFORTABLE:

- Turn down the TV during noisy programs, like shoot-em-ups and biker movies. Close the windows if there are loud noises outside. Loud sounds can actually hurt them.
- Warm a kitten under your sweater or with a heating pad.
- Beds and crates should be placed in a warm, draft-free area of the house, preferably slightly elevated off the floor.
- Occasionally get down on the floor to play with your cat so you're at her level, not a threatening giant towering over her.

48 REASONS CATS HAVE TO BE HAPPY

By Paulette Cooper and David Rudnitsky

If they lie around and nap all day, no one tries to put
   them on Prozac.
Their next door neighbor will never be a member of the
   Manson family...
They don't care if their yachts are big enough...
   or their breasts are big enough...
   or their trust funds are big enough.
They don't waste time standing in line...
   or going on-line.
No one yells at them for leaving the toilet seat up.
They don't worry if Social Security will be around in
   twenty years...
   or if America will be around in twenty years.
Human beings don't make them sneeze.
Catnip hasn't been banned—yet.
Mice are not fattening.
They'll never have to tear off a piece of Saran Wrap.
They'll never have to see the show *Cats*.
They don't have to change their plans at the last minute.
They don't have to change their underwear at the
   last minute.
No matter what happens, they always land on their feet.
They never lose one earring.
They don't have to exercise to aerobic capacity.
They don't have to worry about passing their
   driving test...
   or failing their HIV test.

They don't have to pretend to be interested in opera.

They never receive cold calls from mutual fund salesmen.

If they go to a cat house, no one cares.

No one ever asks them their astrological sign.

They don't have to worry when something black crosses their path.

The Moonies don't try to recruit them.

Their kids leave the house when they're twelve weeks old.

No one ever throws paint at them for wearing a fur coat.

They're not bothered by poor posture... or poor relatives.

When their hair stands on end, they don't have to run to the beauty parlor.

They have nine lives.

No one keeps calling them at dinner hour to ask them to change their long-distance service.

They can fall asleep without melatonin.

They'll rarely have to go to the Betty Ford Clinic.

They don't have to remember the names of Elizabeth Taylor's husbands.

The Psychic Friends Network never sends them bills.

They don't have to get the top off a childproof bottle.

They don't have to videotape all their possessions... or taste a strawberry Slim Fast... or hold their stomachs in at the beach... or sterilize their contact lenses...

They never have to look for a nail file... or a computer file.

They never have to appear on the Jerry Springer show.

They never have to *watch* the Jerry Springer show.

4. Stopping Your Cat From Attacking You

7 Secret Signs Your Cat Is Going to Attack— Maybe You!

Some cats not only attack the hand that feeds them, but the one that pets them. It's often hard to tell, however, whether they really *will* attack or whether they're just posturing. But the following are signs indicating that a cat is not just fooling around.

A change in mood: Tufts University Veterinary School's newsletter, *Catnip,* points out that cats ready for combat show a significant mood change; for example, they'll suddenly appear to be angry or frightened.

Spitting and arching: Cats often spit when they want something, or want someone to stay away. But if they also arch their back or their fur rises while they're spitting, it may mean they're going to attack.

A quick **flick of the tongue** over their lips may show they're becoming agitated.

BE CAREFUL OF YOUR CAT'S BELLY

A cat that rolls over and gets in a belly-up position for you is showing that he trusts you. It's not something he would do with a stranger, since this position makes him very vulnerable.

But don't test just how much he trusts you by touching, petting, or trying to massage his belly. Being touched on the belly may make him suddenly realize how vulnerable he is, triggering his survival instincts, and leading him to attack.

Ears forward mean they're on the offense. Backwards indicates defense.

Whiskers forward and possibly bristling is also a sign of impending attack.

A twitching tail or rippling body can show that they want whatever is going on to stop—and that they might do something to ensure it. Generally, the faster their tail is moving, the more agitated they are.

Raised or curled lip: Although this is usually associated with dogs about to attack, it's something to watch out for in cats as well.

SIMPLE TRICK STOPS CAT FROM CHASING, LEAPING, AND ATTACKING YOUR HANDS OR YOUR ANKLES

Do you have a cat that likes to attack your hands as you play with him, or leap after your ankles as you pass by? Pet therapist and author Dr. John C. Wright offers a simple solution.

He points out that cats are more likely to react to something if it *crosses* their field of vision rather than if it's just dropped directly in front of them. Thus, when your cat sees a fast moving object go past his face, he will redirect his attention from you to that object.

Most behaviorists suggest you carry a toy with you so you're always prepared to immediately redirect any attack.

4 Ways to Stop Your Cat from Turning on You

Want to nip nipping in the bud—especially the kind that seems to happen when everything was going so well? Here you are with your little lovemop on your lap, you gently stroking her, she loving every second, and then, wham, all hell breaks loose. Here's how to reduce the chances of it happening again.

1. Don't pick her up where and when you want. Even if you'd like to put her on your lap and pet her while you watch *Jeopardy* on TV, don't jeopardize your safety and the relationship if she'd like to stay in the other room. Pet her *there* if she's in the mood to be petted at all. Alas, you can no more get your cat to do what you like where you'd like it than you can get your children to.

2. The standard way to protect yourself from a sudden attack during a placid moment is to note when your cat seems to have had enough of petting or playing before flouncing off or rudely attacking. Always stop right before that in the future.

CAT BITES ARE MORE DANGEROUS THAN DOG BITES

Cats' mouths aren't necessarily dirtier than dogs', but cat bites have a tendency to become more infected because cats have fine, needlelike teeth. As many as 50 percent of cat bites may become infected because their teeth are almost injecting the bacteria under the skin, while dog bites have a tendency to be open and bleed more, helping to clean the wound out.

If you get a deep cat bite, see your doctor immediately.

If your cat takes about three minutes of petting or playing before she attacks or nips your fingers, stop at two. Or, if she likes ten petting strokes, make it eight from now on.

3. If she attacks or chases you, don't run off. Or, if you're playing with her, and she attacks your fingers, don't move them. Cats are attracted to movement, which is why they go after your fingers or your moving ankles in the first place. Darting away or wiggling your fingers just makes it more of a game. If you stop moving, she often will.

4. Just because you don't move doesn't mean your lips can't. Say something to show your displeasure. Screaming or shouting "no" often helps—you if not her. And it may make her stop, or at least look around with a what-the-heck-did-I-do-this-time? look.

IS YOUR PERFUME OR AFTERSHAVE MAKING YOUR CAT TURN ON YOU?

Wonder why there are times when your cat won't have anything to do with you, or dislikes a family member or friend of yours? There may be "animals" on you in your perfume or aftershave.

Unfortunately, some of these products are developed from wild animals. Not surprisingly, some domestic cats react badly to this, possibly viewing the scent as a challenge. So getting along better or ending attacks might be as simple as changing a brand of toiletry or cosmetic. The safest type to use is a vegetable-based product.

Most people don't realize just how many animals are used in our everyday products. For example, lanolin, which is found in so many cosmetic items, comes from sheep; lipstick may contain the scales of fish, etc. If your cat is sensitive to "competition" or to how his "friends" are being "used," get around it by avoiding animal products.

---

5. Strange Cat Behavior— and How Experts and Cat Owners Explain and Solve the Problems

8 Weird Things Some Cats Eat or Lick

Your face or hair: Your moisturizer, cosmetics, or shampoo could come from by-products of slaughtered farm animals. Change your brand, or wash your face or hair in a little lemon juice or vinegar. Go light so you don't smell like a salad.

Stamps: Cats can be attracted to the glue, which may contain rendered animal parts. Unless you're in the direct mail business, you probably don't have enough stamps around to harm them— although getting the stamps off your cats could be a sticky situation.

How do you lick the cats-who-lick-stamps problem? Don't leave stamps around, or use faxes and E-mail, or chase your cat off your desk.

Photographs: Chemicals used in the processing of film could be attractive to your cat. Like stamps, there probably aren't enough noxious products on the photos to harm your cat, unless you're a professional photographer.

Dirt: If there's no medical problem causing your cat to eat dirt, just make sure the soil—whether from your garden or your house-plants—doesn't contain pesticides, fertilizers, or chemicals.

Concrete, metal, and other weird things: This is similar to the problem of pica in people: an inexplicable desire to eat bizarre items. Why is your cat eating these things? It could be a hormonal problem. Or maybe it just tastes interesting to your cat. Try removing these odd objects and substituting acceptable toys.

Crossword puzzles (newspapers or letters): The ink from the pen could be attracting your cat, so stop being a show-off and do your puzzles in pencil. Or maybe your cat is just rubbing itself on your scent, which you transferred to the newspaper when you were reading it or doing the puzzle.

To see if it's really the crossword puzzles that are attracting him, *Chicago Tribune* pet writer Steve Dale suggests you put the section on the ground without writing anything in the puzzle. "If your cat is still interested in the crosswords, you have a Mensa cat. Perhaps she'll help you with seven across."

The above are all non-food items that cat sometimes inexplicably eat or lick. Here are two food products some cats flip for—or at.

Olives: No problem if there are no pits. Experts believe it's the preservative in the jar that attracts the cat—plus the fact that some cats like food they can bat around before eating.

Ice cubes: The texture and temperature also seem to make ice cubes a popular item for cats to eat and play with. Again, it isn't harmful.

5 Weird Things Cats Sometimes Do

Silent meowing: Cats actually *are* speaking—only we can't hear it. As Dr. Bruce Fogle, British animal behaviorist, explains: "The meow is only silent because our hearing is so limited. It is a perfectly good meow to any other cat."

Growling and moving their tails for no apparent reason: Something is probably bothering the cat that we don't know about. "Don't you sometimes get a pang of pain or an itch some place when you can't scratch?" asks Fogle.

Cuddling blankets and soft objects: Dr. Michael Fox, in *The New Animal Doctor's Answer Book,* explains that cats weaned too

---

CATS WHO SCARF DOWN WOOL

Some cats eat wool, especially Siamese and Orientals, who you would think would be attracted to silk instead. But devour wool they do, and generally it doesn't harm them, although occasionally it can cause serious blockages.

No one knows if wool-eating is caused by premature weaning, separation anxiety, or lack of fiber in the cat's diet. While they figure it out, owners of wool-eating cats should take action:

- Give your cat lots of fiber.
- Encourage them to eat grass instead, by buying small grass plants.
- Dr. Katherine Houpt, at Cornell University's College of Veterinary Medicine, suggests that you put perfume and hot pepper sauce on something you don't want your cats eating. Then, they will come to associate the smell of the cologne with the evil taste of the pepper and avoid all objects that smell of that cologne. After that happens, spray all your wool items with the same cologne.
- And if all else fails, hide your woolies!

---

early may crave a pacifier, walking around with it like Linus and his blanket. Some people buy the real thing for their cats: baby pacifiers for them to suck on.

5 REASONS CATS BITE ONE SPOT ON THEMSELVES

Biting and licking at the same spot, creating a lick granuloma or "hot spot," is a very common problem. Many cats get sores on those spots, and may even pull all their fur out there, often requiring medical treatment. Why do they do this? Some psychological theories first:

- Insufficient weaning is a common cause, since it's seen most frequently in cats taken away from their mothers too early. This is probably also true for cats who suck on thumbs—theirs or their owners'—which appears to be another variation of this problem.
- Stress may lead to this behavior, as happens when something in their environment has been changed.
- They're just plain bored.
- They've got an obsessive-compulsive problem. As to why they have that, ah, there's the rub—and in this case, not only the rub but the biting, the licking, and the sucking.

The biting problem may instead be the result of an allergy to items such as the following:

- Fleas. This is the most common reason.
- Flea products.
- Environmental allergies.
- Food. This is often hard to determine since a cat can be eating the same food for years and then suddenly develop a problem.

The best thing to do if your cat begins biting and licking himself in one spot is to speak to your vet. He may not know why your cat is doing it, but he may give him some drugs to control it.

Licking themselves before a storm: This is not just an old wives' tale. Leonore Fleischer, author of a delightful book written many years ago called *The Cat's Pajamas*, writes that before an electrical storm the air is charged with static electricity, and a cat's fur is dry, so it attracts dust particles. So, before a storm, cats really do dampen and clean their fur.

Acting as if they've heard something: They may have heard something you didn't, since they can hear the ultrasonic sound of rodents when we can't hear a thing. We should only worry if we can hear something they can't.

The Midnight Crazies—or What's It All About, Fluffy?

"A sudden crash. It could be a lamp falling over or the trash can tipping to the side. Out of a cloud of dust comes the thundering sound of hoofbeats as the feline night stalker races across the entire house, up one wall and down the other... lets out a chest-beating MMRRROWL... and begins its run again... leaps straight off the ground, and pounces down with all its might." That's a great description of the midnight crazies in *Understanding the Cat You Love,* by Mordecai Siegal, who is also the author of *The Cornell Book of Cats.*

He's not the only one to write about this problem, or wonder about it. Here are some possible explanations for this odd behavior, which seems to occur at dusk—the natural time for a cat to hunt—when the sun starts to set, or later when it's altogether dark.

- Cats are nocturnal creatures and are just getting out their pent-up emotions that built up during the day.
- They may be reverting to a wilder state.
- Although they may be acting as if they're a few kibbles short of a full bowl, they may actually be responding to something you can't feel, see, or hear, like a draft on their whiskers from a small crack in the wall, or a movement you didn't see. Or perhaps they smelled a rat—or another cat outside.

Questions Most Often Asked Cat Therapists— and the Answers

We spoke to Carole Wilbourn, famous cat therapist and the author of several cat books, including the lively *Cat Talk*. Here are the most common questions that clients ask her—and the answers.

"I have two cats and my husband and I are divorcing. How should we divide the cats up? If one cat is clearly warmer to you, and the other to him, then each of you should take the cat you're closest to.

"But if the two cats are closer to each other than they are to either of you, then you should find them a loving home together where they can both continue their companionship, because that's how they would be happiest.

"We are introducing a new cat (baby or dog) into our family. What should we do about our cat? Triple your attention to her. Keeping up a running dialogue, making sure she feels included in all activities. "I'm going out now with the baby. Want to come out too?"

"Whenever I eat, my cat jumps up on the table. What do I do? Be consistent. You can't say 'Yes, you can stay up here' some of the time, and 'Get off the table' other times, because how will the cat know what to do? The best solution for centerpiece cats is probably 'Out of sight out of mind.' Take him away when you're eating.

"Also, tie his meals into yours by feeding him at the same time you eat so he doesn't feel deprived.

"What about a cat who plops himself on my book when I'm reading? He just wants to be part of what you're doing. The book may feel good to him. It's also a game to him. He is getting your attention and becoming part of the action.

"The solution is to take yourself to another room, get him to leave by waving a toy at him, or sit in a position that makes the book inaccessible to him.

"I HAVE TWO CATS. SHOULD I TREAT THEM EQUALLY? No. Reinforce the dominant or top cat. He needs to be in charge, so let him be. Which one is the top cat? Usually it's the one you had first. Sometimes it's the cat who wants to be the dominant one.

"WHY DOES MY CAT PRESS RHYTHMICALLY AGAINST ME? It's called kneading and cats are reliving the interaction and comfort they had when they were getting milk from their mothers. They do it as adults when they're insecure and want to feel good, and they do it when they feel good to feel better. If it really bothers you, try to distract them with a towel or sweater to press against instead of you.

"MY CAT KEEPS BRINGING ME MICE AND BIRDS. WHAT DO I DO? Obviously it's not the gift from Tiffany's that you were hoping for, but you mustn't let your cat see how upset you are or get angry with him. He's doing what he instinctively should do.

"How do you stop a cat from being natural? Be calm, don't scold, and try to get the mouse or bird away from him alive so you can release it."

Curtain Climbing and Toilet Paper Unraveling

Curtain climbing can be a serious problem, since it can tear out a cat's nails, and it can even be curtains for a kitten who is knocked out or smothered by the draperies.

Excellent suggestions on how to handle this and many other cat problems were collected by Cindy Tittle Moore, who put together a number of postings into an FAQ on a major cat-lovers' Internet newsgroup called rec.pets.cats.

- If the curtains are light, use tension rods to hang them so they will fall on top of the cat if she tries to climb them. Be sure the cat can't be smothered or injured afterwards.
- Take the drapes off the hooks and thread them barely strong enough to hold them up, so they'll fall down if your cat climbs them. Be sure the cat can't be injured afterwards.
- Buy vertical blinds instead of lace or open weave curtains. They're easy for a cat to look through and don't collect as much hair anyway.

As for **toilet paper,** you can:

- Put the roll so the paper hangs between the roll and the wall.
- Get a cover that rests on top of the toilet paper, or make your own cover.
- Mold aluminum foil to cover the roll, and remove it when you need the paper.
- Balance a small paper cup full of water on top of the roll.
- Put an aluminum can with pennies on top of the roll, so they make noise when they fall down.
- Give up and close the bathroom door.

6. Strange Behavior of Cat Owners

10 Unusual Gifts for Your Cat and Yourself

Underpants for Your Cat: Joybie's Piddle Pants are perfect for cats in heat or for incontinent cats. Machine-washable, in several colors and sizes. Prices from $18-$25. Paws and Claws, 1-757-539-9642.

Catnip from Around the World: 6 samples of catnip from Alaska, Africa, Asia, etc. $14.95 + $3.00 s/h. 1-800-822-8647.

Catnip Blowing Bubbles They're safe and fun for you and your cat. $4.95 per bottle, plus $2.00 shipping and handling. Call 212-691-3279.

Cards for Cats Pictures of cats from 100 years ago saying things pets want to say to their owners, groomers, and fellow pets.

The Litterature catalog has 100 greeting cards: each card is $2. Litterature, RR 1, Box 1234, Grafton, NH 03240. Or call 1-800-639-1099.

My Cat's Story Your cat's baby book/scrapbook keeps records of your cat from kittenhood onwards. It's a 9 x 12-inch album, perfect for you and your cat to share. $20.98 plus $4 shipping. Available from Deartracks, 14415 Hawthorne West, Lake Forest, IL 60045.

Cat credit card A Ralston-Purina Mastercard with your cat's face on it? Call 1-800-386-2722.

Cat Passport Make it easier to travel with your cat by documenting his vital statistics, including personal and health information, in a convenient and official-looking format. It's $6.95 + $3.00 shipping from Castlemain, Inc. Call 1-888-760-4730.

Self-cleaning litter box A microprocessor-based self-cleaning litter box from LitterMaid has an electric eye which automatically sifts the contents of the litter box after your cat has exited it. $199.95 + $16 shipping/handling. Call 1-800-992-2966.

Kitty Kondoms The name tells it all. This gag gift comes in packages of three for $10.85 including shipping/handling, from 1-800-647-8273 or AC Press, PO Box 216, Spring Grove, MN 55974 or http://www.acpress.com

Cat vacuum cleaner Pet-Vac II, Variety International, 18 Technology Drive, Irvine, CA 92718. (714) 727-3646. $19.95.

WACKO CAT NAMES

Pets' Names of the Rich and Famous, by Robert Davenport, is a fun book containing hundreds of names of celebrity cats, like...

Eartha Cat (Roger Caras's cat)

Bing Clawsby (Michael Feinstein's cat)

Joan Pawford and Kitty Dearest (Sally Struthers's cats)

Zsa Zsa (Eva Gabor's cat)

The Butt of the Cat Joke, or the World's Weirdest Cat-Related Story

Sir Isaac Newton is said to have invented the cat door, but at least one person probably wishes that no one had ever invented the modern cat flap. He tried to enter his own home through one, became stuck, and ended up with his buttocks painted.

PLASTIC SURGERY FOR YOUR CAT?

No, cats aren't getting face-lifts and nose jobs yet, but some plastic surgery is being done on cats. For example, a cat with a broken jaw can have its jaw made attractive, and protruding teeth brought into line.

- A cat whose tongue was partially burned off after chewing on a wire had his cheek and mouth built up on one side so he could chew and so he would look better.
- Skin grafts are being done on cats.
- Some Persians have folds taken out of their skin if they irritate their eyes.
- Really fat cats sometimes have the skin around their vulvae removed if they're urinating on themselves.

Coming next: collagen lips for better kissing?

This odd story, reported by *Der Spiegel*, began when a forty-one-year-old man mislaid his keys and tried to crawl back into his house through the cat flap. He was spotted by a group of student pranksters who removed his trousers and pants, painted his bottom bright blue, stuck a daffodil between his buttocks, and put up a sign claiming this was an essay in street art and asking for money.

People assumed it was performance art and that his screams of protest were just part of the act. When he called for help, they would say "very good" and "very clever" and throw coins at him. He was supposedly stuck for two days—which is as hard to believe as the rest of the story—and he was only released when an old woman complained to the police about the noise and they came and released him.

How Cats Can Improve Your Marriage

Many studies show that owning a cat or other pet is physically good for people, lowering their blood pressure and conferring other health benefits. Other studies show that cats help people psychologically.

One psychologist has pointed out that cats also provide interpersonal benefits and improve marriages. Dr. Elayne Kahn of Miami told us: "I know of many marriages which have stayed together because of the children, but there are also many marriages which stay together because of the cat or dog.

"The pet provides continuity and conversation for the couple, something to care for and love together. A cat is a continuing source of happiness that gives the 'parents' something to talk about with each other and with others."

She added, "Unlike children, cats don't go through adolescent or adult rebellion. And even if the couple's children didn't turn out perfectly, in their eyes, the cat probably did."

HAS YOUR CAT SENT YOU A CARD LATELY?

If your cat has sent you a card, and you "helped" pick it out, don't be embarrassed. More and more cats are buying their "mothers" cards. In fact, two of the top twenty humorous Mother's Day cards from one of the largest card companies, American Greetings, were "sent" from people's cats.

A popular Mother's Day card from a cat was "The top ten reasons I put up with you." It included examples like: "You've finally learned what kind of food I'll eat," and "You know better than to try to give me a bath."

FIND YOUR INNER PURR

It is said that if you purr with your cat, it will soothe the both of you, strengthen the human-feline bond, and make you as relaxed and contented as your cat. Who says this? The people who sell a tape for you and your cat to listen to in purr-fect harmony. This guided relaxation experience combines the sounds of cat and human purring with new age musical background. Imaginer Communications, Cherokee Station, P.O. Box 20721, New York, New York 10021 or 1-800-949-0688. The one-hour Cat Lover's Guide to Relaxation is $9.95.

Survey:

Who Is Better Looking: Your Cat or Your Significant Other?

"No contest. Cats are the best-looking creatures on earth." (Rachelle Pachtman, New York)

"I don't have a significant other now, but when I think of my past ones, I'd have to say, my cats." (Monica Pignotti, New York)

"All cats are much more beautiful than any human I've ever seen. Humans are so funny-looking with their furless skin." (Stacy Young, Oregon)

"I don't have a significant other but my cat is pretty damned cute."

And votes for the spouse or significant other:

"Husband. His whiskers never grow as long as our cat's, thank goodness."

"Significant other. I do not have a death wish." (Sandy Krinsky, California)

Cloning Your Cat: Could You and Should You?

One day you may be able to clone your cat, but would you end up with one identical to yours?

Perhaps the clone would be similar in appearance, but not in personality. There are powerful prenatal influences that determine a cat's personality along with environmental factors, such as treatment by other cats, siblings, animals, and people—especially you, her owner.

Even if you could clone your cat, it would remain very expensive—and don't wait around for the breeders and geneticists to start doing it inexpensively for you. They probably won't be that interested, because they're primarily concerned with improving the standard, not with duplicating it.

7. Kitty Litter Blues and Why Your Cat Won't Use It

10 Reasons Your Cat's Not Using the Litter Box—and What to Do About It

The number one difficulty for most cat owners concerns the litter box. So here are the major problems, questions, and answers.

WHERE THE LITTER BOX IS:

Animal therapist Dr. John Wright says the three requirements for a successful litter box are: location, location, and location.

When choosing the place for a litter box—or if you're trying to find out why your cat won't use it—consider the following:

- Escape routes are needed. When cats are using the box, they may feel vulnerable and want to be able to flee if they choose. That may be why some cats won't use covered or hooded boxes; they can't see to get away quickly.
- It must be away from food and water. Cats don't like to excrete in their "hunting" (food and water) areas.
- It must be accessible to older cats. Construct ramps so older cats can get in and out of the litter box easily.

HAVING ENOUGH LITTER BOXES:

- In a multilevel home, you should have boxes on every floor of the house.
- In a multi-cat home, there should be one more litter pan than the number of cats.
- If you're having litter-box problems, put several small litter boxes with different brands of litter in a few locations. Cats will choose the one they like best, and you can move that box later to the location you select.

- Some cats like to defecate in one area and urinate in another, so make sure they have a litter box for each.

The right litter in the right amount:

- Outdoor cats who occasionally urinate indoors may prefer outdoor dirt or sand in the litter box.
- Finer granules in the litter can stick to long-haired cats and to any pet's paws, leading them to avoid the box.
- Some litter products may make cats sick. Some insist—others deny—that clumping litter can lead to constipation and possibly worse.
- Litter made out of recycled newspapers is good for cats who have had recent surgery such as declawing. But introduce this product slowly—not all cats like it.
- Make sure there's not too much litter. Fill the box only with about two to three inches of litter; more could make cats uncomfortable.
- If you've changed brands of litter and introduced it too fast, return to the old and introduce the new brand slowly.

The cleanliness and the smell:

- The litter box should be scrupulously clean. Clear the solids daily and wash the pan out with unscented soap and water at least once a week.
- Extra clumping litter may stick to the pan. Baking soda and pan liners help.
- The top should be removed regularly on covered litter boxes to prevent the buildup of odors.
- Put the litter box on a large piece of Astroturf or a mat to prevent tracking problems.

PSYCHOLOGICAL FACTORS—
OR IS THE PROBLEM WITH YOUR CAT?

Is she unhappy, confused, or under stress? Does she dislike her diet—or her life? Have there been any changes in her life or yours that are affecting her? Has she just been declawed? Maybe there's a new baby in the house, or a new cat, or someone has moved away, left, or another pet has become ill or died. If she's an older cat, she might have bladder or arthritis problems. She may need more attention, emotionally and physically. More playtime, a rethinking of her diet, or a visit to the vet could solve the litter problem.

How to Tell if Your Cat Hates the Litter

Not using the litter is certainly a sign. But there could be other reasons she's avoiding it. If you want to tell if it's because she dislikes it, note whether or not she is digging near it. The happier the cat is with litter, the more she will dig. So, if your cat is digging outside the litter box, chances are, she doesn't like what's in it.

Animal behaviorists suggest that to tell what kind of litter your cat likes best, you set up a second litter box with a different brand and see which box she uses the most and which she scratches the most.

When Your Cat's Aim Is Bad
but His Intentions Are Good

If your cat is trying to use the litter box and just misses a bit, perhaps he's too large for the litter box.

- Try a bigger box.
- Or one with higher sides.
- Or put the litter box inside a larger cardboard box.
- Or place the litter box on Astroturf or newspaper.

Stopping Your Cat from Going in the Bed, Tub, or Elsewhere

- Put the litter box right next to the spot, and if your cat starts using the box there, keep moving the box away until it's where you want it.
- Put plastic over the bed or tub or area where she shouldn't be going.
- Put portions of food on paper plates in the tub, the bed, whatever. That should change your cat's habits since cats don't like to pee where they eat.
- If she's going in the tub, put an inch of water in there so the next time she jumps in, she'll have an unpleasant surprise.

Cleaning Up Accidents so Your Cat Won't Return to the Spot

- Clean accidents as fast as possible.
- Use paper towels first to get up as much liquid as you can.
- Cover the spot with a sheet of plastic.
- Scope mouthwash is said to be good for getting urine smells out of the rug.
- Another product people recommend is Sink the Stink, available is scuba stores.
- Don't use ammonia products, because the smell is too close to urine for a cat.
- Odor neutralizers are better than products which simply mask or cover up the smell, but enzymes (like Anti-Icky-Poo) may take a few weeks to work, and the smell may still be apparent to you and your cat for a while.

8 Ways to Train or Retrain Your Cat to Use the Litter Box

The reason cats can be trained to use the litter box is that it's natural for them to bury their feces to disguise the odor and prevent predators from finding it. Here are some ways you can get your cat to do what is supposed to come naturally.

- When training a kitten, right after each meal, with your hand on his belly, take him to the litter box. He'll know what to do.
- Pick up his fecal matter with a piece of tissue and deposit it in his box.
- Watch him until he seems ready to go—crouched with his tail raised—and quickly place him in the litter box.
- Confine him to a room with food and a litter box.
- If he chooses one location and you prefer another, try moving the box to his place for a short time and then back to where you want it.

YOU CAN SAVE FACE WITH KITTY LITTER

Diane Irons, an international image consultant, tells of another use for kitty litter. "It's a great face mask that only costs a couple of cents instead of the $40 or so that cosmetic companies charge for a little bottle."

She says that all you have to do is mix all-natural (non-clumping) kitty litter with a little water and make a paste of it. Then put it on your face for five minutes. "I know of a very expensive spa that uses it for mud baths and charges their clients a fortune," says the author of *The World's Best Kept Beauty Secrets.*

- Block off a small area and put a clean litter box at one end, and food and water at the other, with toys in between. Confine him there whenever you can't watch him. He won't want to poop or urinate near his dishes, or on top of his playthings, so he will choose the litter box.

- Dr. Peter Neville, one of England's top animal behaviorists, suggests you confine your kitten to a small pen with a bed. Scatter fine kitty litter outside the bed area. The cat won't soil the bed but will soil elsewhere. Once he eliminates in the litter on the floor, put this used litter together on a plastic sheet. Quickly transfer the used litter you've collected to a litter box.

- Don't punish a cat for "accidents."

THE FIRST KITTY LITTER

Cat boxes were filled with newspapers when entrepreneur George Plitt came up with the idea of packaging ashes from burned wood for cats to use. The concept of litter was so new—this was before Ed Lowe popularized kitty litter using clay—that customers didn't know what "litter" meant.

One day an irate customer called Mr. Plitt after buying his KleenKitty product. "I've tried and I've tried," she said angrily, "but my cats refuse to eat it."

8. Disciplining Your Cat (You Gotta Do It Sometimes)

These 15 Things Will Stop Your Cat from Misbehaving

TO STOP A CAT FROM GOING WHERE HE SHOULDN'T WHEN YOU'RE NOT THERE

- Put aluminum foil on the spot you don't want him walking on. Cats don't like the aluminum foil feel on their paws.
- Use double sticky tape there, since cats don't like having their feet stick to something.
- Buy a "Cat Scram" to startle him: an ultrasonic motion detector that sets off a loud alarm only your cat hears.
- Put balloons up so the cat's claws break them. But be sure to spray the balloons with a cat's off product so he doesn't chew on them after they've burst.

WHY PUNISHMENT DOESN'T WORK FOR CATS

When training a cat, you have to praise and reward him for what he does rather than punishing or scolding him for what he does wrong. The reason was spelled out nicely by O'Farrell and Neville in *Manual of Feline Behavior:*

A cat cannot think abstractly or symbolically. It cannot ponder the past or make plans for the future. It is therefore useless to punish a cat for something it did even a few minutes previously...

By the same token, a cat cannot understand the concept of a rule, it cannot follow rules or break rules. House-training, for example, is the result of a combination of classical conditioning and instinct, and not the result of conscientiousness or a sense of duty.

Cats don't like the following smells, so sprinkle, rub, or spray them on something— even yourself if necessary

- Bitter Apple, available in pet food stores and catalogues.
- Vinegar. If there's none around, check an old bottle of wine to see if it's turned.
- Raw onions.
- Diluted lemon, lemon peel, or orange peel.
- Stinky perfume.
- Menthol.

If you catch your cat in a bad act:

- Get a children's bicycle horn and blow it when your cat does something you don't like. It's better if your cat doesn't see that the sound comes from you.

Hiss—Don't Kiss—Your Cat

Most cat lovers think of cats as little people—except for cats! They're more likely to think of themselves as kittens and of us as their mothers—and sometimes they think of themselves as mothers and of us as their kittens.

If your cat does something wrong, and you're a woman, don't whisper sweetly "bad little boy" or give her a kiss or hug to show that "mommy" isn't really all that mad. Your cat doesn't respond to what you say so much as what you do, and the tone of your voice. Your voice should mimic that of her mother's when she was a kitten and did something wrong.

When she was a naughty kitten, her mother hissed at her. Cats "remember" this sound from their past, and they'll usually at least look around to see where it's coming from. And sometimes, just stopping cats from doing something temporarily stops the behavior altogether.

- Stamp your feet.
- Squirt him with a water gun or mister.
- Shout "bad cat" or something similar while stamping your feet, and squirting him with water if you wish.
- Carry toys with you so you can distract him immediately.

Your cat may not immediately get the point with any of these methods, so be patient.

The Rules (for Cats)

"Every profession has simple secrets that somehow never get widely distributed." To let you in on the secrets, here are a few amusing truisms and rules of thumb for veterinary medicine, written by Mike Richards, D.V.M.

- Fluffy really will breed with his sister (mother, daughter, etc.). Cats don't think of these relationships the way you do.
- The neighbors probably didn't poison your cat. Take her to your vet and find out what is really going on.
- Cats hit by cars rarely live to learn from the experience.
- If you don't follow the directions, the medication probably won't work. If you know you won't follow directions in advance, tell your vet. It saves you both a lot of frustration—and may save you money.
- If you bring leftover medications from home, your vet will know you aren't following the directions since you were probably supposed to use them until they were gone.
- Pets are like vacations—they cost at least twice as much as you think they will.
- Declawed cats can be let outside. They just shouldn't be forced to fend for themselves out there.
- Cats don't really need to run free. They're not social animals who need to be with their "pack." If you make room in your life for them, they don't need to seek another family—two- or four-footed.
- Neutered cats don't turn into wimpy sops. Their meow doesn't become three octaves higher, either.
- Children only rarely take care of pets responsibly. Don't expect this. It irritates the child and is bad for the pet.
- All cats occasionally bite. Some just need more provocation than others. Be careful.
- Taking the time and spending the money to treat fleas properly will save both many times over in the long run.

Don't Be Cruel—or Should You Be?

There are many effective ways of handling cats or getting them to behave that some consider to be cruel. For example, when bathing or grooming a cat, people used to put a screen in the bottom of the tub so a cat would dig its nails into it, get stuck, and not move during the ordeal.

Many behaviorists still recommend that you put Tabasco sauce or cayenne pepper on items to keep cats from biting them, or that you put your fingers way back in a biting kitten's mouth so they're sufficiently uncomfortable and stop nipping.

Even America's top animal behaviorist suggests that you put a noxious substance where your cat has messed, pick him up and put his nose close to it, dabbing some on his nose or gum so he develops a negative association between the smell and going in that spot. Is this cruel?

What about those who suggest lightly flicking the kitten's nose or giving him a quick swipe to startle him, as another cat might do with his paw? Mother cats do these things to kittens, so are you being cruel if you, their "mother," flick or swipe as well? Are things less cruel if their mothers did it to them? Is it kind to be cruel if the alternative is sending the cat to a shelter where he will probably die?

The decision is yours.

How Shocking Is It to Shock Your Cat?

Many people think the use of electricity to help keep cats in a fenced area, or to keep them off the couch, is quite shocking. But Ross Becker, editor of *CATsumer Report,* tried an electric shock collar on himself several times and reported that it wasn't all *that* bad. He also stressed that cats have a lot of fur, and don't feel pain as strongly as we do.

But many people still believe that a much larger person administering electric shock to a much smaller pet to change a natural behavior the person finds offensive is a howling shame.

9. Getting Your Cat to Stop Waking You Up, Scratching the Furniture, and Other Hard-to-Handle Problems

How to Turn Off "Alarm-Clock Cats" Who Wake You Up

Something has just woken you up, and it's not your alarm clock. It's your cat who *thinks* he's your alarm clock and that he should decide when it's time for you to wake up. Some solutions to this common problem:

Play with your cat before he goes to sleep at night, so he's more tired in the morning and lets you sleep later. Using catnip toys may make him more rambunctious—and then exhausted—which may make him sleep even later.

Feed him later, before he goes to sleep, so he isn't as hungry in the morning.

Have hateful noises in your bedroom. Would your cat really be so anxious to come in there or stay in there if a vacuum cleaner or hair dryer was running in the room? Keep one next to your bed and turn it on when you want your cat to get out.

Use standard deterrence methods, like keeping a plant mister by your bed and squirting it when he tries to wake you.

Close your bedroom door.

WHY YOUR CAT SLEEPS IN YOUR BED—AND HOW TO MAKE IT MORE COMFORTABLE

Most studies show that most owners let their cats sleep in their beds, but what's in it for your cat? Maybe he chooses to do it because he loves you. (Why not?) More accurately, maybe he does it because he loves your scent.

More likely, though, it's not your sparkling smell or scintillating personality that's attracting him, but the heat from your body. Cats are heat-seeking animals, and your body is warmer than the floor, or wherever else he might choose to sleep.

That may be why, even if you have a huge bed to sleep in, your cat usually chooses the spot right next to you, sometimes crowding you out.

One solution is to put a small heating pad on the far side of the bed. Your cat will find this warmer (and calmer) than you.

Another is to give up and just get a special pillow that holds both of you. This "Cuddly Cushion" is a standard king-sized pillow with a concave area your cat can sink right into, right next to your head. Pillow Pal, $24.95 + $5.50 shipping/handling, 1-888-473-8700.

Teach Your Cat to Stop Scratching and Use the Scratching Post

It's natural for cats in the wild to scratch; since they use their claws for hunting, they need to keep them sharp. Even indoors, cats have a need to scratch, and not just for the exercise. Since they have sweat glands between their paw pads, scratching lets them leave their scent behind, their way of saying, "Kilroy was here."

It's impossible to persuade them not to do it. "You can't teach a cat not to scratch, but you can teach him *what* to scratch," says famed pet expert and author Warren Eckstein.

Unfortunately, what most of them want is to scratch your beloved couch into strings. Here are a few ways to keep cats from scratching where they shouldn't:

- Use standard deterrence methods, putting nasty substances on what they're scratching to keep them away from it, or putting things around that will break loudly, like balloons.
- Decorate with leather and naugahyde instead of nubby cloth, which cats prefer to scratch.

A BETTER WAY TO DECLAW YOUR CAT—IF YOU MUST

Most owners are against declawing cats, for humanitarian reasons (it's cruel); practical reasons (cats need to scratch); life-saving reasons (a declawed cat outside could die); medical reasons (surgery can lead to complications); and psychological ones (how would you like it if someone ripped out your nails?).

For some people, however, it's a matter of declawing their cat or giving him to a shelter, where he will have little chance of survival. These people may want to ask their vet to use a newer technique called flexor tendenectomy. This operation is less mutilating than the old way, and the cat heals faster, although his (shorter) nails will still have to be clipped afterwards.

- Put Soft Paws or caps on their claws.
- Have them declawed if you wish. Fortunately most cat owners don't wish to declaw their cats.
- Trim their nails.

To persuade a cat to use a scratching post, here are some ideas from Warren Eckstein, along with Carolyn Janik and Ruth Rejnis, authors of the comprehensive *The Complete Idiot's Guide to Living With a Cat.*

- Smear catnip on the cat's post.
- Hang a dangling toy from the top of it.
- Move the scratching post so it's next to something they like to scratch.
- Put the carpet nap-side-out on the scratching post, since some cats prefer rougher surfaces.

ARE SOFT PAWS AN ALTERNATIVE TO DECLAWING?

Soft Paws are like little caps for your cat's nails, preventing your cat from embarking on a scratch-and-destroy mission. The downside is that:

- They're not permanent, and you have to put them on every few months.
- Not everyone can use them. "If you can trim your cat's nails, you can apply Soft Paws at home," Tyler Stratton, the marketing manager told us.
- If you can't do it, the procedure has to be done by a veterinarian, which costs money.
- At first, cats may shake their paws a lot or try to bite the paws off, but they do eventually get used to it.

Before you let these minor drawbacks scare you off, though, remember that the alternative, declawing, must be done under total anesthesia, and is expensive, dangerous, and cruel. Soft Paws is definitely a better way to go for those who cannot live with a scratching post. (Contact Soft Paws at 1-800-433-7297.)

- Guide her paws over it, showing her what to do. (Some experts think this idea can backfire, turning cats against scratching posts permanently because of their abhorrence of being manipulated.)
- Make the scratching post a pleasant place for them to go by putting their toys or a treat nearby, or even a smelly old sock there. You might also play with your cat near the post.
- Try a log instead of a scratching post.

WHAT RADIO PROGRAMS DOES YOUR CAT LIKE BEST— AND SHOULD YOU CALL YOUR CAT WHILE YOU'RE AWAY?

It's not a bad idea to leave a radio on for your cat during the day while you're away. But what type of program would your cat like best? One that has sCATalogical humor, like Howard Stern? Will your cat RUSH for Limbaugh? Does Imus give him morning sickness?

Talk show stations—whatever the subject matter—are probably best, since human voices will give your cat the feeling that people are around, even if he can't see them.

We've also heard of people who call their cat during the day and leave a message on the answering machine so the cat hears their voice while they're gone.

We think this would confuse as many cats as it would comfort ("I hear Mommy but I don't see her"), but we don't know, because so far we can't find anyone who admits to doing it. Stay tuned…

Leaving Cats Alone All Day

Warren Eckstein coined the term "latchkey cats" for our four-legged friends who are left at home all day. Warren stresses that cats left alone—especially very dependent ones, such as some of the exotic breeds—without sufficient distraction or stimulation can become stressed, and even physically ill, with psychosomatic ailments. If you go away all day, consider his suggestions for keeping cats from becoming bored and sick.

Make your cat's toys more interesting: Rather than just leaving toys around, hide them so your cat can look for them, or alternate the toys so he won't get the same old ones each day and get bored with them.

Let him look outside: Buy a cat hammock or perch, or just put together an el-cheapo kind—a secure table with a pillow on it pushed against the window.

Leave him something "smelly": Something that smells of you (hey, we're not implying anything) can be heaven for your cat. One man wore a T-shirt to bed each night so he could give it to his cat the next day when he went out. He called it "baking" the

SEND YOUR CAT A SMELL LETTER

If you're going away for a while, Dr. Michael Fox suggests you send your cat a "smell letter," to comfort your cat when he doesn't have you and your familiar scent around. To make it, take a piece of paper you've rubbed on your forehead, hands, arms, and lightly under your armpits and mail it to where he's staying.

What should this "smell letter" say? It depends on whether your cat can read.

shirt. But anything you've worn (or sat on) would probably work well, without your having to cook up anything special for your cat.

You can also give your cat your sheets and pillowcases before you put them in the laundry. Let your cat sit on them when you go out so he'll have your beloved smells with him when he can't get the real thing. In fact, you can put down any soft fabric for them, except wool; why tempt them unnecessarily?

Get your cat a companion: Bear in mind that some cats would be more stressed and distressed over the competition for your affection than they would be mollified by the company of another cat while you're gone. Therefore, don't automatically assume that a second cat is always the best solution. Consider also that, if you have a very affectionate cat, some of that warmth and attention may be transferred toward a second cat and away from you.

10. Saving Money on Cat Items (or Lowering the Tab on Tabby)

How to Save Money on Cat Food

By the time a cat is five years old, you will have spent an average of almost $1000 feeding her. Here are a few ways to save some money:

Buy better, not cheaper foods: You often have to give cats more of the generic inexpensive foods to get the same nutrients contained in the premium brands, so you're not saving money by buying the cheap stuff.

Avoid supercolossal jumbo sizes: Buying perishables in huge quantities can be a waste because food spoils, and then you're throwing away your "savings." In some foods, vitamins deteriorate and mold forms, so don't buy more than a month's worth at a time.

Buy dry food and make it taste better: Since moist foods consist of as much as 75 percent water, switching from moist to dry costs less and supplies more nutrition ounce for ounce.

Unfortunately, your cat may try to outsmart you because dry food isn't as tasty, so he may turn up his cute little nose and refuse to eat it. You can try to tempt him by mixing it with a small amount of the more expensive (tastier) moist food, or do other things to make the dry taste better. For example, there are supplements that can be sprinkled on dry food to make it more palatable, or sprinkle a tiny bit of the liquid from your tuna-fish can, and watch your cat's attitude towards kibbles change.

Persuade the checkout clerk you're going to eat the cat food yourself: One of our thriftier friends has actually done this. Since cat food is safe for human consumption, and stores can't charge sales tax on food for people, he persuades the checkout clerks that he plans to eat the cat food himself, and saves the sales tax.

He once had to open the box of kibbles and prepare to eat one while he was in line to prove to a sales clerk that it was for himself, but the saleswoman was so horrified, she decided not to challenge him in his claim and sold it to him without the sales tax.

Is this a good idea? Is it legal? Is it honest? Are we really suggesting it? Nah...

How to Save Money When Buying a Cat

- Not surprisingly, right before Christmas is the worst time to buy a cat—and right after Christmas is often the best.
- Random breeds and adopted grown cats are less expensive than purebreds and pedigreed kittens.
- Among purebred and pedigree kittens, a cat intended for showing or breeding costs more than one that will only be a pet. So if you're not planning to show or breed her, let the breeder know, and you may get a bargain.

How to Save Money on Cat Litter

The first and most obvious suggestion is to buy in quantity—but where do you keep the litter then? Storage problems prevent many people from buying in money-saving bulk.

One cat lover came up with a good idea: put the extra kitty litter in the bottom of one of your large garbage bins. This extra weight also prevents your cat from tipping the garbage over—often a big problem—and hides and holds the litter, assuring that you will always have extra litter around if you need it.

The second suggestion was posted to a CompuServe forum by a cat owner who explained that she saved money by making her own litter with old newspapers, which she then ran through a paper shredder. Since cats like to scratch, she mixes this with a little bit of nonscoopable, inexpensive generic litter. Incidentally, kitty litter made of newspapers is also available in stores, but, of course, costs much more money than the homemade variety.

How to Save by Making Your Own Toys for Your Cat

Cat toys are expensive! And an inexpensive homemade toy can bring him just as much—or more—pleasure as a motorized mink mouse. Here are some cheap alternatives.

- Take a stuffed toy and put it in bed with you the night before you give it to your cat. With your scent on it, your cat will be almost as happy as with a new catnip-scented toy.
- Liven up old toys by smearing catnip on them. Or, smear catnip on an old sock you were going to throw away, or put a bit of catnip in it and sew it closed.
- Turn the lights down, and shine a flashlight around the room so the beam dances. Your cat will happily pounce on the glow.
- Give your cat a box to leap into after you've taken the gift out—and leave the tissue still inside the box for him.
- Put small objects like marbles in an empty tissue box with the opening taped over. Cut a paw-sized hole in the side of the box and rattle the box in front of your cat. This is one of the many suggestions in *51 Ways to Entertain Your House Cat While You're Out,* by Stephanie Laland, a book for people with bored cats.
- Put a hole in a newspaper and peer at your cat through the hole. Then let your cat happily pounce on the paper.

Your cat will also enjoy playing with things you already have around the house like

- Ping-Pong balls,
- empty grocery bags,
- champagne corks,
- empty spools of thread,
- logs from outside (make sure there are no bugs on them before you bring them in),
- a piece of paper rolled up in a ball.

How to Save Money on Vet Bills

One emergency treatment from a vet can cost more than everything you buy for your cat for a year. Here's how to reduce the bill:

- Be alert to possible problems or changes of behavior during the day, so you don't end up having to get expensive emergency care late at night.
- Ask your vet if your cat can recuperate at home rather than at the clinic or hospital. It's often better for your cat and always cheaper.
- Find out how much treatment will cost before you consent to it, especially in serious situations in which there may not be much hope.

$4,500 IN REWARDS

The Humane Society of the United States, in an attempt to help stop the abuse of animals, has posted the following rewards:

- Up to $2,000 for information leading to the arrest and conviction of any person who willfully poisons, mutilates, or tortures, or attempts to poison, mutilate, or torture, any dog or cat.
- Up to $2,500 for information leading to the arrest and conviction of any wholesale dealer in dogs and cats who knowingly buys or otherwise procures any stolen animal.

- Get a second opinion before letting your cat undergo expensive treatment.
- Choose a reasonably priced hospital or a veterinarian's office with emergency-room facilities before you need it, and have the number ready.
- Find out in advance the time and day that emergency room rates go into effect in your vet's office.
- Take your cat to the vet for annual checkups.

- If you let gum disease put the bite on your cat, it could take a healthy chunk from your wallet later. Brush your cat's teeth regularly.
- Keep your cat groomed and her nails clipped so you don't have problems later.
- If your cat needs to be spayed or neutered, look for places that do it less expensively. Call Spay/USA at 1-800-248-SPAY.
- Get pet health insurance. If you have more than one cat, ask if they offer a discount.
- Learn how to treat simple non-threatening problems yourself.
- For poisoning, call animal poison control hotlines.

3 Ways to Save Money on Program and Advantage

We're not recommending the following; we're just telling how some people save money on these popular flea products.

Apparently products like Program, Advantage, and Frontline have identical formulations for cats as for dogs—only the dog products may cost less. For example, Program for cats is identical to Program for dogs, except the latter comes in pill form and is cheaper.

One woman wrote on the Internet that dog Program comes in three sizes, and the large one, split in half, serves two cats for a month. She also found it easier to give her cats a pill than a liquid.

Second, some of these products cost less in larger quantities, so people buy them that way and split them up themselves. For example, one person posted that the only difference between the sizes of Advantage was the dosages and the prices; the ingredients and concentration were exactly the same. She bought a larger package and split the dosages up according to the size of her cats.

Finally, one person wrote that they purchased an over-the-counter alternative flea product called "Zodiac" for far less money.

SHOULD YOU USE PROGRAM, ADVANTAGE, FRONTLINE, ETC.?

Should you use products like Program or take advantage of Advantage? Not according to *CATsumer Report,* which points out that if there's any danger of reinfestation of fleas, you have to use these products with another insecticide. So why subject your cat to any more chemicals than necessary?

These products are like birth-control pills for fleas. They won't get rid of existing fleas, or stop new ones from coming into the house, but they will stop your cat's fleas from mating. They take a long time to work, don't work well in heavily infested situations, are difficult to give your cat, and are expensive. "It's only a simple cure if you have a simple problem," they wrote.

Survey:

Would You Give Up Your Cat for One Million Dollars?

A few people would not; some would, but only with reservations; and the only ones who said they would were men. Here's one who wouldn't:

"Nope. Not a chance. Some things can't be bought. One of them is the joy of having a relationship with a cat."

Some would give up their cats for a million dollars, but with conditions:

"Yes, in a minute. But I'd like fifty-nine seconds to think about it."

"Yes, because I know he would give me up for a million dollars."

"As long as I could give him to a neighbor or a very close friend."

"Yes but only if I got visitation rights every other weekend."

A few uncertainties:

"One million? Uh, would that be income or capital gains."

"I don't have to answer now, and I reserve my right to decide later [smile]." (Jerry Whitfield, Florida)

And two men who would:

"Yes, but I'd probably hate myself in the morning."

"One thousand for mine." (Ted Mayett, Nevada)

Save Money on Grooming Emergencies

Matted hair can lead to problems with parasites and skin disease, so don't let this problem get too serious—at which point it can also become very expensive. If you can't get the mats out easily and painlessly yourself, spend the money and go to a professional groomer. But first you might try the following:

Corn starch poured over matted areas is said to make the fur softer and easier to comb.

Peanut butter: One cat lover on CompuServe claimed that rubbing peanut butter into the mat loosened the clumps and made them easier to get rid of.

Ice cubes sometimes work. If you harden the mat with cubes, you may be able to untangle it with more ease.

A **mat splitter** is a must for tough areas.

A **knitting needle** of the kind you use for dropped stitches has been helpful in detangling knots.

Should You Save Money by Vaccinating Your Own Cat?

Yes, you *can* buy the necessary items and do it yourself. You can also save a lot of money that way, especially if you have more than one cat. But as Dr. Daniel Jacoby of Forty-third Avenue Animal Hospital of Phoenix, Arizona asked: "Would you vaccinate your own child for measles if the pharmacist provided you with the vaccine and syringe?"

No, you wouldn't, and here are a few other problems and dangers Dr. Jacoby pointed out that you may face if you try vaccinating your own cat, plus two important things to remember:

- Severe allergic reactions can occur when a cat is vaccinated and immediate attention from a veterinarian may be needed or your cat could die.

- How are you going to know if the vaccine was handled properly before you bought it?

Do Indoor Cats Need Rabies Shots?

Can you save money by not having your cat vaccinated for rabies? If that's what you're planning on, think about this:

There have been more reports of rabies in cats than in dogs in the United States.

Even if you have an indoor cat and don't think you have to worry, what makes you think your cat will never ever get outdoors? (Won't he ever go to the vet?) And what makes you think another animal—such as a bat—will never get into your house?

One more thought on this subject: If you don't have your cat vaccinated, and he gets rabies, not only will he suffer, and you suffer, but others could suffer as well. According to *Feline Practice*, one rabid kitten in a pet store had contact with more than six hundred people, almost all of whom had to get painful rabies shots.

JUST HAVING A CAT MAY SAVE YOU MONEY

It's not just cats' abilities as mousers, or the reduction in possible bills for marriage counseling and psychiatrists (since cats make their owners happier) that may save money. Medical bills among cat owners are actually lower. One English study found that when people were given cats, their general health improved—which led to fewer medical visits.

This was confirmed by a Medicare study of one thousand elderly Americans. Pet owners reported fewer medical visits than those without pets.

- Are you sure your cat is healthy enough to give the vaccine to? Some vaccines, if administered to an unhealthy animal, may be ineffective, or even harmful.

- How are you going to safely dispose of the hazardous material afterwards?

- You may be bitten or badly scratched by your cat while trying to inject him.

- Your children can pick up the needle and get hurt.

These should be some pretty good reasons to think carefully about it, but if you're going to do it anyway, here are two rules that are very important:

Rule number 1: Watch your cat for a couple of hours after the vaccination for signs of breathing problems or vomiting, and if there is a problem, get him to a vet right away.

Rule number 2: Only vaccinate your cat during the day when your veterinarian's office is open. If there's an emergency, and you have to race your cat to the vet when his office is closed, it will no doubt cost you a lot more than you tried to save by doing it yourself.

It can also be very traumatic. As one woman learned who had to race her cat to the vet late at night after a bad reaction to a home-administered vaccination: "It was a long scary drive … at 11 P.M. with a hyperventilating, puking cat."

How to Make Money in Cats

Here are some professions and areas suitable for cat lovers: cat breeder, cat sitter and home boarder, cat groomer, pet taxi company, veterinarian, veterinary assistant, veterinary technician, veterinarian's secretary or office manager, cat boutique, cat mail-order catalog owner, cat therapist, cat photographer, cat psychic, animal control officer, shelter manager, kennel boarding or operator, grief counselor, cat cemetery, cat book dealer, cat writer.

11. Food and Your Cat

The 4 Types of Meals Cats Like to Eat

There have been many experiments and studies—not surprisingly often done by cat food companies—on food preferences in cats. Here's what they found your cat likes best:

Smaller meals, more frequently: In the classic study in this area, when cats were allowed to eat whenever they wanted to, they returned to their feeding bowls an average of thirty-six times each day. So feed your cats less food but more frequently.

Fish over meat is their general preference, although not all cats like fish.

Novel diets: Cats get bored—and sick—if always fed the same type of food.

THE 4 THINGS CATS REALLY WANT WHILE EATING

- **To eat undisturbed.**
- **To be fed at the same time and place each day.** Otherwise, it's stressful to them.
- **To eat from immaculately clean bowls** with no scent of cleaning agents.
- **Not to have their whiskers touched when they eat.** Cats don't like to have their whiskers disturbed, and some won't eat out of a bowl whose sides touch their whiskers when they eat.

If your cat is acting oddly when she eats, perhaps taking the kibbles out of the bowl and eating them elsewhere or suddenly refusing food after you've bought her a new bowl, check to see if her whiskers are touching the sides.

Foods of different shapes: According to Ralston-Purina, some cats prefer one shape to another. That's why dry kibbles are formed in a variety of different shapes. Cats also have "mouth feels," so some foods feel better in their mouths than others.

Is Moist, Semi-Moist, or Dry Food the Best?

Moist food is the tastiest for cats, but it's high in fat, expensive, smelly, and contains preservatives.

Semi-moist is less smelly than moist, usually lower in fat, more expensive, and also contains preservatives.

Dry is the least tasty for your cat, but the best for his gums and teeth, the lowest in fat, has the least smell, and is the cheapest and easiest to prepare.

What About Baby Food for Your Cat?

Your cat may be your little baby, but don't give her a regular diet of baby food, because it doesn't meet feline nutritional needs, according to *Catnip*. Most of the meat varieties of baby food contain only meat, and cats need vegetables and minerals as well.

Another problem is that many baby foods contain onion powder in large quantities, to make them tastier to children, but onion powder has been shown to cause anemia in cats. Unfortunately, most baby-food companies won't tell you how much onion powder they add, but if there's none in the food, they may be glad to tell you that!

20 People Foods Cats Should Never Eat

Uncooked bread dough can cause gastric bloating and severe intoxication from the fermentation. Go to a vet immediately if your cat eats bread that was cooling and rising.

Baby food (see sidebar)

Onions: The flavor of onions can increase the palatability of foods, so onion is sometimes added in tiny amounts to cat foods. In large amounts it can be toxic because it contains a chemical that can harm red blood cells.

Cooked goldfish? You see all those jokes about cats eyeing goldfish, but eating goldfish may not be a joke. (It also may not be a people food, except for the occasional one swallowed by college kids.)

According to *Canine and Feline Nutrition* by Case, Carey, and Kirakawa, goldfish contain an enzyme which destroys thiamin (vitamin B1), although there is no danger from their eating just one goldfish.

IS CANDY DANDY FOR YOUR CAT?

Recent studies show that cats do prefer sweetened dishes, but since it's no great cat-astrophe to them if they don't get a sugar fix, why give them what can hurt them? Sweets can led to cavities and even diabetes in older cats.

The problem is that you may not know if a food has sweetener in it because it may be listed as corn syrup, molasses, beet sugar, fructose, or sucrose. Look on the label for those names and avoid them.

As for chocolate, as little as a sixteen-ounce candy bar can kill a cat. The darker and more bitter the chocolate is, the more dangerous. By the way, cocoa can also be toxic to cats.

Raw fish: In large quantities, they can also cause vitamin deficiencies, especially carp and salt water herring.

Cooked fish should only be given to cats occasionally because there are too many toxins from pollution in them right now.

People tuna is not a complete and balanced diet for cats, and can make them sick if fed regularly to them. Furthermore, canned tuna is frequently packed in salty brine or fattening oil.

Are Rawhide Chews Safe for Cats?

Rawhide bones are generally associated with dogs, but more and more people are giving the smaller ones to cats, especially teething kittens. Is it safe for them?

It depends on how they chew them and where you buy them. Don't let your cat or kitten chew them down to the last few inches because small pieces can get stuck in their throats.

You also have to be careful where you buy them. You can sometimes find them at flea markets and outlet places, but these were most likely purchased cheaply from foreign countries— countries that may cure raw cattle hides with arsenic, which may still linger in the bones.

Cheap rawhide bones may also be contaminated with insect eggs or come from the hides of water buffalo, which have a lot of fat. Or they may even have been washed with water that has high trace elements of mercury. So only buy genuine 100 percent rawhide bones from a respectable and reliable pet place.

As for cat tuna, buy the high-quality tuna-flavored cat food, not the cheap kind, which may have a lot of fat in it. Furthermore, the better tuna is supplemented with extra vitamin E.

Milk or cream can be dangerous even in small quantities. Adult cats are usually deficient in lactase (an enzyme that breaks down lactose), and they can't digest dairy products properly. As for kittens, cow's milk is very different from cat's milk, and doesn't meet the nutritional needs of kittens. They can't metabolize it correctly, so if you give them milk, use lactose-free milk.

Cheese contains too much fat, and like milk, can cause diarrhea.

Raw or undercooked eggs can lead to salmonella, but scrambled eggs are all right if well cooked. Raw egg whites can destroy certain vitamins, which can lead to skin problems. No Caesar salad for Fluffy!

Liver should be reserved for rare occasions—no more than every ten days—and should never be given rare or partly raw, which can lead to hypervitaminosis. Liver flavoring is fine for cats.

Fish bones are more dangerous to cats than any other bones.

Turkey and chicken bones are also to be avoided, unless they've been put in a pressure cooker, which takes the brittleness out of the bones. Then turkey and chicken bones can be good for your cat, especially the marrow.

Table scraps should be avoided.

Seasonings and preservatives: Fur-get about it.

Fats, salts, and sugars—all the good stuff: The same things you shouldn't eat—fatty, greasy, salty, and sweet "comfort foods"

---

6 PEOPLE FOODS YOUR CAT CAN EAT

In addition to your cat's regular diet, here are seven people foods you should feel free to share with your cat:

- Plain boiled meat or chicken (no bones)
- Yogurt
- Air-popped popcorn (no butter or oil)
- Boiled egg (1 tablespoon only, hard-cooked preferred)
- Boiled vegetables (a tiny amount only, or it can cause gastrointestinal problems)
- Cooked liver

like hot dogs, bacon, fried foods—can cause obesity, tooth decay, and digestive problems in cats.

A totally vegetarian diet is impossible for cats, who are carnivores and require meat and fish regularly. If you are a vegetarian, don't try to convert your cat!

Candy and chocolate: (see sidebar)

Caffeine: Avoid giving coffee, cola, tea, and other caffeinated foods to cats.

Dog food: Although this is not a people food, we've included this here among no-goes for cats. A diet of only dog food can result in blindness in cats because it doesn't contain enough of an amino acid called taurine, which is essential for cats, and is now added to commercially prepared cat food. A diet of dog food can also lead to cardiomyopathy and death from heart failure.

Of course, there are exceptions to every rule. America's most long-lived cat shares his breakfast with his owner: bacon, eggs, and coffee with cream. And both owner and cat are doing just fine, thank you.

12. Food Problems— and Is Your Tabby Too Tubby?

3 Odd but Common Eating and Drinking Problems

Drinking water from a faucet, shower tap, or toilet instead of their bowl: Cats are attracted to movement, so lapping up water from a drippy faucet may be more of a challenge to them than drinking water that's just sitting there in a bowl doing nothing. To a bored cat, pouncing on the water dripping from an active faucet must be the feline equivalent to our playing something like Pac-Man.

GRASS- AND PLANT-EATING CATS

Actually, a cat eating plants isn't so strange, for in the wild, cats get their vegetables and fiber by eating the stomach contents of their prey. A plant-eating cat is getting these nutrients now from primary instead of secondary sources.

Most cats like the taste of grass, and it's good for them, aiding in their digestion, and it contains needed folic acid. Most importantly—especially for long-haired cats—grass helps them regurgitate fur balls before they cause intestinal blockages.

You can buy grass commercially in little pots, grow your own, or pick some pesticide-free grass from the garden.

If their little game really bothers you, then fix your faucets so they don't drip, or leave a little water in the basin or tub so their paws get wet, which they generally don't like. Alternately, put deterrent-type products in the area, such as double-sided sticky tape.

Drinking from a toilet is a different concern, for the cleansers you may have used there could make it dangerous for your cat. You might just have to keep the bathroom door closed or the lid down when you're not around to supervise.

Turning the bowl over: Your cat may be telling you something, so listen up. Is their water stale? Is there something wrong with the tap water in your area, like too many chemicals? If there's a problem, take care of it.

Scattering food around: *Cat Facts* says your cat may be scattering his food because he has too much. Try giving him less dry food, or if it's moist, cut it up to make it easier for him to eat.

He may also be doing it because he's bored, so find him something else to do. Give him more toys to play with, or more time playing with you.

Handling Finicky Eaters and Hunger Strikes

Warm the food slightly: Cats like food at room or mouse temperature, so spend a few seconds microwaving your cat's food, especially dry food. If it's moist food, before you open the can, warm a little water in a bowl and put the can in it for a few minutes after you take it out of the refrigerator.

Add "people" juice: You can make food tastier—and often irresistible—by adding a little of the liquid from such things as cans of clams. You can use the clams afterwards to make spaghetti with clam sauce.

Hand feed her: She may take food from your hand that she's rejecting from a bowl.

Exercise her before mealtime: In the wild, hunting for prey makes cats hungry, so let her chase a mouse toy for a while before you feed her.

Smear her food on her: If it's moist food, put a small piece on your (clean) finger and wipe it on the side of her mouth. She'll probably lick the area clean.

Mix new food with her old food: Don't feed her something new or something she doesn't like all at once. Add the new food slowly to the old, or alternate dishes so she's getting what she likes for one meal, and the new food for the other, for example, canned food for dinner and the boring dry kibbles for breakfast.

Buy smelly stuff: Generally, the more food smells, the more cats eat it.

Finicky Drinkers or Is Your Water Safe for Your Cat?

Here are a few things to watch out for in your water, as described in *Save Our Planet: 750 Everyday Ways You Can Help Clean up the Earth*.

Color: An orange or red hue may indicate contamination from rusting pipes.

Smell: A smell like rotten eggs, a sweet candy-like smell, or an oily gas-tank smell should alert you to a problem.

Sensations: If you feel a tingling or burning sensation while drinking the water, or you get rashes afterwards, watch out.

If anything is suspect about your water, what should you and your cat do?

- Drink non-tap water, which is best for cats anyway.
- Contact your local water company and ask for their most recent analysis.
- Use a home lead test to test if your water is free from lead.

---

5 FOOD AND WATER BOWLS THAT MAY NOT BE SAFE FOR YOUR CAT

- Bowls made outside the U.S.
- Antique bowls
- Those made by children at school
- Any bowl cleaned with cleansers and not carefully washed afterwards
- A plastic bowl with scratches in it

Vomiting or "Bulimic" Cats

"Bulimic cats" is a term that's sometimes jokingly used, but if your cat vomits frequently, it's not a joke. A little vomiting can be healthy, and is nothing to be alarmed about. If it's happening a lot, Dr. Carin Smith, author of *1001 Training Tips for Your Cat,* suggests you put the food in different places to slow down the feeding, since your cat will have to walk around to get the food.

Also, feed your cat smaller meals. If he's vomiting fur and hair, put petroleum jelly or a commercial remedy on his paw or the side of his mouth so he licks it off.

Your cat may also be vomiting because he's allergic to his food, in which case you'll have to try different diet. Or he may be throwing up because you're feeding him cheap food, in which case the solution is obvious.

You should also consider the possibility that your cat is vomiting not because of his stomach but because of his teeth, which may be so bad that he can't chew his food enough to digest it properly.

One last word on this: if your cat is vomiting up a piece of string, don't pull it out. Take him to a vet immediately, since you could tear his intestines trying to get it out yourself.

How to Tell If Your Feline's a Fatty— and Does It Matter?

Politicians may look for fat cats but most people don't want them—with good reason. A recent study of two thousand cats found that tubby tabbies had a four-and-a-half times greater chance of developing diabetes, were seven times more likely to require veterinary care for lameness, and were three times more likely to have skin problems, probably because they couldn't reach all the parts of their bodies to groom themselves.

Worst of all, fat cats were twice as likely to die in middle age.

This isn't an occasional problem, either, for about 25 percent of all pet cats in America are overweight—and 5 percent of those are *really* fat.

How can you tell if your cat fits in this category? The unscientific way is to check whether you have trouble breathing if your cat is sitting on your chest.

Or try the touch and see method. A cat whose weight is healthy will have a waistline. To find it, feel your cat with both hands, working backward toward the tail. At the end of the cat's ribs there should be a slight indentation. Overweight cats will have a bulge from that point to the tail.

An overweight cat will generally also have a stomach that hangs, plus a roll of fat over the ribs. Run your hands lightly over your cat's rib cage and see if you can feel those ribs.

The scientific way to tell if your cat is too fat is to compare his weight to what the experts say is correct. Most books on specific breeds will tell you what your type of cat should weigh. If he's not a pedigreed breed, ask your vet what his weight should be. Then, to find out your cat's weight, step on a scale while holding him. Then let your cat go and weigh yourself without him. The difference is the weight of your cat.

How's that for scientific?

How to Diet with Your Cat

Few owners can resist giving their furry little friends some tasty between-meal treats. But some pet foods, like some people foods, are too high in fat. Alas, for both people and cat food, fat's what makes it taste good.

If both of you have a problem, try to diet together, using some of the same techniques for your cat that work for people.

Eat less calories and fill up on fiber: There are high-fiber cat and people foods, which provide a feeling of fullness with little fat.

Choose low-fat foods: Fat in cat food ranges from 5 to 30 percent. Don't try to cut fat out altogether since your cat needs fat to fight off infections, heal wounds, metabolize vitamins, and for a better coat.

Don't change to a low-fat diet all at once: Gradually convert, so both of you have a chance to get used to it.

Feed your cat smaller meals: Frequent feedings of three or four small meals containing the same amount of foods as you were doling out in less-frequent feedings may help reduce hunger pangs and make both of you feel as if you're eating more.

Avoid crash and starvation diets: They're dangerous for both of you.

Keep a written record of weight loss: Set a goal and note patterns of eating when it shouldn't occur.

Eliminate unplanned snacks: Your record should include the time and place for meals. Both of you should stay away from the dining area when you're not eating a regularly scheduled meal.

Exercise more: Try to give your cat games to play that require more motion for both of you. For example, when he comes to you, start to run after him, or go in the other room and call him, and then chase him when he comes.

Measure food portions: Keep to the guidelines. Look at the labels and see what they say. For example, generally a ten-pound cat should only be eating a half a cup of food a day.

Use non-food treats for rewards: When you've lost weight, let yourself read something that interests you or do something you enjoy for an extra hour. When he loses weight, buy him a new toy.

THE KOSHER KAT

Since household cats are often considered family, are they of the same religion as their owners? Do they have to follow the same dietary laws? What does one do in situations in which certain types of food aren't allowed in the house, and your cat likes to eat them?

These problems sometimes arise in religious Jewish families, and here's what Rabbi Neil Cooper of Beth Hillel-Beth El Temple in Wynnewood, Pennsylvania says:

- "There's no reason why you can't make your cats homemade food from kosher meat instead of canned meat if you don't want to bring *traif* into your house." (A few companies produce specially formulated tinned meat and fish products for the kosher cat.)

- "Since cats tend not to eat much dairy anyway, not mixing meat and milk probably won't be a problem."

- What should you do about your cat's food if you fast on Yom Kippur, the Day of Atonement? "There is no stricture against your *handling* food, only eating it, so you can serve food to your cat. As for their eating it, they can. Since animals can't 'atone,' there is no reason why they should have to fast, too."

- Passover poses unique problems, because the household must be cleared of all products not kosher for Passover. "Some folks 'sell' their pets to a non-Jewish neighbor or friend for the Passover holidays, and 'buy' them back afterwards."

- "You can make your own food for your cats to eat over Passover that contains no grain."

Use regular food as treats: Save your dessert not for the end of a meal, but for when you want to reward yourself. For your cat, take the regular kibbles out of his food and give him that as a reward, but make sure he doesn't get any extra food.

Avoid temptation: Stay out of your kitchen when possible, and don't keep a lot of fattening things in your refrigerator for your sake. Keep your cat from sitting on the counter or even being in the kitchen while you prepare your dinner. He'll be tempted to beg, and you'll be tempted to give him something.

13. What You Should (But Probably Don't) Know about Cat Food Cans and Labels

8 Phrases That Mean Nothing on Cat Food Labels

100 percent nutritious: Says who?

Natural: Naturally what? Anyone can call anything natural. Actually, what's natural to a cat is a rodent, so purchased cat food can't be natural, says *Catnip*.

Herbal ingredients: Which ones do they contain, and why are they better than nonherbal ingredients?

Organic: There's no legal definition of the term.

Light: It could actually have more calories in it than a product that isn't marked that way.

No added preservatives: That just means no preservatives were added when the cat food was formulated, but there could have been some already in the ingredients that they used.

Entrée: Whose? What does that word mean to your cat?

Gourmet: Can have the same ingredients as any other complete and balanced food—except you'll probably pay a lot more when this meaningless word appears on the label.

WHAT COLOR IS YOUR CAT FOOD?

First of all, if your cat food is very red, you don't want it. They put that color in for you, not for your cat. And you don't want it for your cat because it's potentially dangerous. The color comes from sodium nitrate—which is found in such foods as hot dogs and bacon—and it could be a carcinogen.

The manufacturers don't have to tell you if they are using sodium nitrate, but they'll probably tell you if they're not. Call the company. There should be an 800 number on the package.

Incidentally, what color would your cat food be if the manufacturer didn't color it in some way? Probably black. Some cat food, by law, has to be covered with charcoal to make sure no one sells pet food as people food.

The 5 Things to Look for on Any Cat Food Label

According to *Catnip,* the best cat food labels should read:

"Feeding cats" or something similar, like "substantiated by feeding studies" or "tested with feeding trials," should be on the label. Otherwise the product was not tested by feeding it to cats.

Taurine: Make sure it's been added to the product, because cats need it to prevent blindness.

Animal Ingredients: Like people food, ingredients that are most plentiful are listed first. Make sure animal ingredients are right up there at the top.

The acronym "AAFCO": This stands for the Association of American Feed Control Officials, the group responsible for enforcing regulations concerning pet food.

Complete: The word can't be used unless the food really is complete and meets dietary requirements. The best thing for it to say is "complete and balanced for all life stages" because that means it has met the most stringent requirements.

SURPRISE! PLAIN OLD CHICKEN MAY BE BETTER FOR YOUR CAT THAN CHICKEN "DINNERS," "ENTRÉES," OR "PLATTERS"

If the can just says "Chicken," then according to *Catnip,* it must contain at least 95 percent chicken.

But when the label says "chicken dinner" or "chicken platter" or "chicken entrée" or something similarly fancy, there only has to be 25 percent of the ingredient featured in the title. Incidentally, just because it says "dinner" doesn't mean it's balanced.

WHAT'S "PULLTABITIS?"

Don't look in your medical dictionary for this because the word doesn't exist. Unfortunately, the problem does. It first came to light when someone revealed on the Internet that she had been severely injured and ended up in the hospital, now suffering permanent nerve damage, because she cut herself with those infuriating little pull tabs on cat food cans.

Next thing you know, other people wrote in that they too had suffered severe injuries from it, and others pitched in with their suggestions on how to open the cans without cutting your finger off.

- Use a pot holder.
- Forget the tab altogether and use an electrical can opener all around the rim.
- Choose products with lighter tops. You're likely to do less damage.
- Pull the tab off with a spoon.

14. How to Make Fleas Flee

The Single Best Flea Product (and One Approved for Your Cat That Could Kill Him)

Never dismiss the problem as "Well, I only saw a few fleas." If you see five fleas on your cat right now, there may be ninety-five of them in various stages of development that you will unfortunately see or feel one day if you don't do something about it today.

What is the best flea product? Certainly not Deet, as some would guess. Deet actually can cause severe side effects in humans—mostly children—and should be avoided for animals also. Stick instead with products from the pyrethrum family. These are natural insecticides derived from chrysanthemums.

The pyrethrums come in many forms, and *CATsumer Report* said the best for cats was Pyrethrins. These are packaged with an enzyme inhibitor. Read the label, and don't spray cats with any product that has more than 1 percent of the enzyme inhibitor and 0.15 percent of a pyrethrin product.

But be careful. *Permethrin*, a synthetic version of pyrethrum, is indisputably the best anti-flea and tick product for people and dogs. (If you're worried about Lyme disease, this is the product to buy.) But cats are enormously sensitive to permethrin—it can even kill them.

Not only should you never put permethrin on your cat, even though the label may say nothing about that, but if your cat plays with a dog, your dog should not be given permethrin either. The literature has reported cases of permethrin toxicity in cats who slept next to treated dogs.

A Few Fascinating Facts about Fleas

- These miniature vampires are among the deadliest animals in the world. They have started epidemics—like the dreaded bubonic plague—in which infected fleas on rodents passed on the bacteria when they bit humans.
- Just four female fleas feeding four times a day for 100 days will bite your cat 1,600 times.
- A female flea will consume fifteen times her own body weight in blood a day.
- There are thousands of known species of fleas.
- Cat and dog fleas are closely related, and cat fleas may be found on dogs.
- A flea can jump the equivalent of a person jumping over the Statue of Liberty.
- Fleas fed on dinosaur blood 180 million years ago.
- Fleas may have played an interesting role in the history of pets. Some believe that the popularity of small lap dogs could have occurred because of fleas. Before the advent of pesticides,

---

DO ELECTRONIC AND REGULAR FLEA COLLARS WORK?

Not really, so you can probably do without both. As for electronic collars, studies have shown that they *don't* repel fleas, affect jumping rates, interfere with reproduction, or change the development of fleas.

Regular flea collars only work for a little while. So, why bother, since you'll probably need another, more lasting solution later? Do you really want to expose your cat to so much insecticide? Furthermore, these ineffective or halfhearted methods leave cat owners with a false sense of security that they're doing something, which gives the fleas a head start at reproducing and causing problems.

fleas were such a terrible problem that women may have chosen small dogs to distract them. When holding the small dogs to their chests, or on their laps, they discovered that some of the fleas went to the dog instead of to them.

Wear White Socks to Find Out If Your Cat Has Fleas

If your cat has fleas, it's as likely that your house *doesn't* as you are to encounter an alien this year. One way to tell if you have a problem (with fleas, not aliens) is to walk through your house with white socks on. If there are small black specks on your socks afterwards, you have fleas.

Dr. Herbert Salm, a retired veterinarian in Connecticut, suggested an interesting way for people to tell whether or not the little tiny black specks they may see around the house, or on their pillow, are really flea droppings: He says to pick up these pepper-like pieces, put them on a white piece of paper or white napkin, and put a little water on them. If the speck turns red, it's a flea dropping filled with blood.

If you suspect fleas on your cat, and you have tiny bites below your knee, they're from a flea. They prefer to feed on that area.

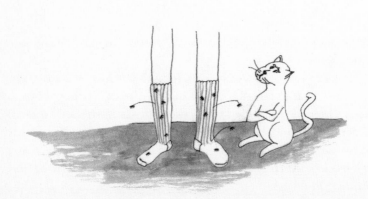

15. How to Talk to Your Cat— and Vice Versa

How to Talk to Your Cat So She Will Listen

What's the right tone of voice to use when talking to your cat? Some behaviorists suggest you use a different tone depending on what you're doing and what you want to happen. Playing with your cat? Petting her? Use a sweet, higher-pitched, almost purring voice. Cats respond well to the higher frequencies, which is why they generally respond better to women's voices than to men's.

Whistling also causes an interesting reaction in some cats. Try it at different pitches, whistling different things: one note, a tune, repeated higher, whatever. Some cats yawn or have a strange reaction, depending on what you're whistling and what pitch it is, but usually there is some reaction and most do sit up and listen. So, in some cases, if you want your cat, just whistle.

What Your Cat Is Trying to Say to You

One good meow is worth a thousand words—and your cat has a lot more than one good meow. An oft-cited study found that cats have sixteen different sounds, which are divided into three groups: murmurs (purring sounds); vowels (meows); and "strained intensity" sounds (like hissing and screaming). Put them all together and a cat is believed to be able to make over 100 different sounds.

Just because a cat doesn't speak your language doesn't mean he doesn't speak *a* language. And just because you don't understand his body cues doesn't mean he isn't telling you *something*. Sounds are only one way your cat talks to you. The position and movement of his tail, eyes, ears, whiskers, and more, are also saying things like "I'm scared" or "I like this" or even "Enough of this nonsense already."

A cat may also be telling you something with his body. He may hear your keys jingling, recognize that you're going out, and immediately leap toward the door so he can get out too. The rattle of silverware or the odor of some food may be a signal that you're making dinner for yourself, and he will race into the kitchen with a silent "me too."

Some experts believe that cats have the communication abilities of a one- to two-year-old child. Therefore, think of your cat as an adorable child who hasn't learned to speak words yet, and uses other methods to communicate.

Secrets of Purring, or "I Purr, Therefore I Am"

DOES PURRING MEAN A CAT IS HAPPY? No, it doesn't have any emotional connotation. For a kitten, purring starts off as a homing device. When he's just a few days old, his mother purrs, he feels the vibrations and then knows where to find her so he can nurse. Afterwards he purrs while she feeds him so his mother knows he's getting his milk.

CATS WHO TRY TO "TALK" TO YOU
WHEN YOU'RE ON THE PHONE

Does your cat ever come over to you when you're on the phone? That's because she sees you talking, doesn't see anyone around, and thinks you're talking to her.

How you're talking to your caller may determine whether your cat decides to join in. Dr. Steve Aiken, America Online's Pet Shrink, says that "if the person you're talking to on the other end is a salesperson or someone you don't want to talk to, your cat will probably stay where he is. But if you're talking to someone in warm and loving tones, then your cat may come over, thinking that loving is meant for him."

BUT KITTENS DRINKING MILK ARE HAPPY AND RELAXED, AREN'T THEY? Happy, yes, but getting milk is very hard work for them.

DO CATS PURR WHEN THEY'RE UNHAPPY? When they're sitting on your lap and purring, there's no doubt that they're content. But there are times when cats purr just as earnestly and loudly, and they're miserable.

IS THERE ANY TIME WHEN CATS DON'T PURR? While they're sleeping.

ARE THERE ANY UNUSUAL TIMES WHEN CATS PURR? Cats sometimes purr when they're in labor and in intense pain. Some even purr when they are dying.

DO CATS PURR WHEN THEY'RE AROUND OTHER CATS? Dominant cats purr when they're approaching inferior cats. Cats may also purr when they're sick and other cats are around, perhaps so the other cats won't take advantage of their infirmities and attack them.

WHAT CAUSES PURRING? There are several theories, but the most accepted is that cats have false vocal cords, and air passing over these probably makes those delightful sounds.

There is simple support for this: when your cat is purring, put your hand on his voice box region, and you'll feel purring coming from the larynx.

16. Your Cat's World— and Can She See It on TV?

What Your Cat Can See, Hear, Feel, and Taste

What cats see: When cats look at something, to them it's like looking through a frosted glass or a window that is steaming up a bit. Cats don't have a good sense of detail, although they can see slight movement very well from a distance. They also have good peripheral vision, and can see to the sides better than we can.

What colors they see: Cats can see colors, but they appear far more washed out to them than to us, and they can't distinguish between some colors. For example, to them, all snow is probably yellow (!) and it's believed that they see objects in more gray and green tones than we do.

You won't see a cat choosing to play with a brightly colored object over a dull one because they just don't care much about its color. After all, they hunt in twilight and darkness, and the shade of the mouse doesn't make any difference in the way it tastes to them.

What they can hear: Cats can hear high-pitched sounds that match the high pitch of mice, who can hear even higher ones than cats.

Cats don't like loud sounds, such as jackhammers. (Who does?) Their hearing is so supersensitive that they can distinguish between two sounds whose sources are only a few inches apart. Unfortunately, they start to lose their extraordinary auditory abilities around the age of five.

What they can feel: While cats are so sensitive to heat that a kitten can find his mother by the warmth of her body, their paws are insensitive to temperature, enabling them to walk in deep snow.

What they can taste: Cats do like sweets and they're also very sensitive to bitter foods, capable of tasting bitter flavors in the most minute quantities.

Cats are also believed to have a special taste for the flavor of water, which is why some cats won't drink it if it has been treated with chemicals or is in a dish that has been washed with such water.

If you don't buy special water for such sensitive cats, use a filter on tap water, or let it sit for twenty-four hours before serving, so the chemicals sink to the bottom.

MUSIC AND YOUR CAT: DOES SHE LIKE PURR-CELL AND MEW-ZART?

O Sole Me-ow! Here are some facts about music and your cat.

- If you start singing off-key, your cat may meow in distress.
- Mice sing—some badly—and one experiment showed that cats were attracted to mice who sing off-key.
- A certain key makes kittens defecate but may sexually arouse adult cats. (We'll tell you the note if you promise not to test it out for yourself: It's E in the fourth octave. Don't write us about the results. We don't want to know.)
- Cats may respond to some music, for example, becoming happy when they hear the theme song of a TV show.

Can Cats Watch TV and See in Mirrors?

Cats react to mirrors and television when they first seem them, and some cats think their reflection is another cat and hiss or spit at it, or even try to go around the back to see what's inside. Indeed, some cats will even urinate on a mirror, possibly thinking a sexually available or aggressive cat is in there.

Although they are initially attracted to the movement that they see in mirrors and on television—cats are fascinated by any perceived prey that moves—most cats eventually come to ignore reflected or electronic images, especially mirrors. Since what's in front of them doesn't smell like another cat, they habituate to the images and lose interest in staring at mirrors or watching TV. Many cats do like watching some cat videos whose content is aimed at them.

Cats that sit and watch TV with their owner may be responding not to the program itself but to the fact that their *owners* are responding to the television set. TV time for many cats is a time when their owner's hand may be free to stroke them, when their owners aren't doing very much, and may therefore pay more attention to them. So cats come to associate TV time with happy time for them, and respond positively when the set is turned on.

As for mirrors, Cornell University's Katherine A. Houpt, D.V.M., Ph.D., said that pets "don't seem to recognize that it's themselves." When we asked her why, she replied diplomatically, "Some people feel they're not intelligent enough."

She suggested that the following could prove these people wrong. Try to put something on your cat's head without her realizing it, and set her in front of a mirror. If you've gotten that far, and she looks in the mirror and tries to swat the object off her head, she realizes she's seeing herself in the mirror, that the object is on her head. She's also a genius.

WHY CATS ARE SO MUCH ALIKE

Did you ever wonder why there are so many breeds of dogs, whose sizes and shapes are so different, while most cats are quite similar? Dogs have been domesticated for over one hundred thousand years, while cats have only been domesticated about 6,000 years. Some animals would not be able to recognize their remote ancestors, but the basic structure of the cat is pretty much the same.

So, will your cat one day be bigger than an Afghan (the throw as well as the dog), have more spots than a Dalmatian and more pompons on it than a show poodle? Probably not. Cats are not as genetically variable as dogs. While you might change a leopard's or a cat's spots, you won't change his shape. Except for eye color and fur color and length, all cats are basically the same, and will be, for the next few hundred years anyway.

Why? Some people think it's because the cat is already perfect. (Purr-fect?)

5 Things Your Cat Knows about You

The following amusing description of what our cats know about us was written by Dr. Daniel Jacoby of Forty-Third Avenue Animal Hospital in Phoenix, Arizona.

You are bigger than they are: This they discovered the first time you accidentally stepped on them.

You are a great source of food: And it must amaze cats, who no doubt see us as ponderous, clawless buffoons with a bowling ball's brain and a physique to match, yet every day we supply them with tasty cat food.

You are easily manipulated: Walk a mile in your cat's collar and you'll see that you are the proverbial pushover. Your needs as far as your cat goes are simple: the desire to be loved; the desire to sleep undisturbed, and to figure out your taxes without meows, yelps, and howls from the help of a furry-footed paper-scattering critter.

You are slower than they are: They can click on their power-booster jet rockets and fly into another room in a blur and hide in a spot in your house you don't know exists and can never find.

You aren't particularly bright: A cat knows the true meaning of life, but he's not sharing the secret with us—he knows when he's got a good thing going.

Survey:

How Many People Would Rather Be on a Desert Island With Their Cat Than With Their Significant Other?

The results? About even. A few samples:

"Cats, because they like to cuddle, forgive you easily, and let you know right away if you've done something wrong—not like some men who don't like to cuddle, hold grudges, and months later tell you something insignificant that you did wrong." (Deana Holmes, Utah)

"Cats, because there would be no conflicts as to who would sweep the sand out of the lean-to or change the toilet paper leaves. Besides, the cat could catch and share the dinner." (Annette Friedman, New Jersey)

A few in-betweens:

"Which human—and what's happening to my cat in the meantime?"

"Depends on what the human looks like."

"Unless the human is great, I'll take my chances with my cat."

And some votes for the significant other:

"I'd rather be with my husband. If I sent him out to hunt, he wouldn't come back with a mouse." (Barbara Gidaly, New York)

"A man. Red-blooded, all-American men make me purr." (Marrille Fendelman, New York)

"Spouse wins. You can only discuss politics and world news and gossip on a limited level with a cat. Besides, they make a lousy date."

17. If You're Allergic to Cats or Have Multiple Cats

What Every Cat Allergy Sufferer Should Know

WHAT ARE YOU REALLY ALLERGIC TO? There's a saying that cats aren't really that clean because they're covered with spit! It's usually not the cat's long hair which causes allergic reactions but the protein in your cat's saliva—which is all over your cat. When your cat licks himself, that protein floats through the air on "dander." This dander—sort of like dandruff—causes some people's immune systems to overreact.

HOW LONG DOES DANDER LAST? Weighing about one-tenth of what household dust weighs, dander hangs around in the air for years. It's been found in houses ten years after a cat has been living there.

HELP COMING SOON FOR THOSE ALLERGIC TO CATS

An incredible one-third of all people who own cats are allergic to them. Who are the best known sneezers and wheezers? President John F. Kennedy was allergic to his children's cat; and President Bill Clinton is so allergic, it is said that he has to have regular allergy shots in order to live with Socks.

Soon, there will be a new allergy treatment that works far better than existing methods, in a shorter period of time, with considerably less discomfort. Allervax Cat will be administered by injections (sorry about that), but just a few of them—two to four plus boosters—instead of the slew of shots that's given now.

Studies have shown that Allervax-C relieves 75 to 87 percent of cat-allergy symptoms after just one week, depending on the strength of the dosage. What more could you want? Hmm. No injections. 100 percent success. Immediate relief....

WHEN YOUR CAT IS THE ALLERGIC ONE

Fifteen percent of all cats are allergic, with allergies to flea bites being the most common problem. Food allergies are another biggie, as are inhalant allergies, and cats may be allergic to chemicals in your carpet or shampoo, to products like wool, or to house dust or outdoor irritants, such as tree pollen and ragweed.

Allergy symptoms might include hair loss and sores, sneezing, coughing, tearing, or diarrhea. Food allergies generally show up as skin disorders.

Remember that cats with one allergy often have others, so even if you get rid of one problem, you may have to start working on the next one. Since allergy problems can be complicated, and hard to diagnose and get rid of, you might want to find a cat allergy specialist if you're having no luck with your local vet.

IF YOU'RE NOT ALLERGIC NOW, COULD YOU BE LATER? People's bodies change, and you can develop allergies to your cats even after years of exposure to them. Allergies are more likely to occur after you've been away from your cat for a while. On a happier note, some people—especially children who have cat allergies—have them disappear in time.

ARE SOME CATS BETTER THAN OTHERS FOR ALLERGIC PEOPLE? Since the allergen is found in cat spit, a cat that cleans itself can be a worse problem than a less-fastidious one. Also, certain breeds may be better for some allergic people: cats with short or no hair, like the Cornish rex or Devon rex. The Japanese bobtail is said to be good. Some think the sphinx, which has almost no hair, would be good, but they have oily skins, so that discounts that theory.

DOES GROOMING A CAT HELP? Yes, but brushing your cat can also make the dander float around in the air, which can make your symptoms worse. So either use a pet vacuum, groom your cat outdoors, or bring him to a groomer.

WHAT ABOUT "WASHING" A CAT? Some experts say it helps if you run a washcloth with distilled water and no soap over your cat at least once a week.

WHAT TYPE OF VACUUM CLEANER WORKS BEST TO REMOVE DANDER FROM A CARPET? An upright is better than a canister vacuum. Use the beater brush that comes with it. Triple filters or "HEPA" air cleaners are recommended. And use sticky tape on the furniture to pick up lint and hair.

IS ANY LITTER BETTER THAN OTHERS FOR ALLERGIC PEOPLE/CATS? Litter made of recycled newspapers is good. Watch out for litter with deodorants or fragrances, which can be a problem for allergy and asthma sufferers. Get litter with as little dust as possible.

WHAT ELSE CAN YOU DO TO HELP ALLEVIATE ALLERGIES?
• Wash your hands after touching your cat. • Replace your draperies and rugs with blinds. • Get rid of shag carpets. • Wash floors with sponges and wet mops. • Install filters. • Keep your cat out of the bedroom. • Take allergy medication. • Wait for Allervax to come on the market.

Read This If You Have More Than One Cat

Half of all households with cats have two or more, and while that gives owners at least twice as much pleasure, sometimes it also presents double trouble. Here are some problems people have encountered, along with solutions, some from *CATsumer Report*.

My two cats are on two different diets. How can I keep them from eating each other's food? Two possibilities. The obvious solution is to feed them at the same time but in separate areas with a door closed between them. Remember to alternate the rooms you put the cats in so one isn't getting second-rate treatment (in his eyes).

Secondly, there is a new feeder called "The Smart Bowl," which comes with a collar you put on the cat that you don't want going near the food in the "wired" bowl. If he approaches the bowl, it lets out a loud shriek. Then you can come over to the cat and do the same. (The Smart Bowl, 1-800-891-2695. $39.95.)

If all of my cats eat the same food, can I put it all in one bowl? No, because even if they eat the same thing, they may not like the same kind of bowl. Furthermore, cats like to eat in different places. And finally, with a communal bowl, it's hard to tell if one cat isn't eating sufficiently and needs to be watched. So put down different bowls in different places in your house.

Should my cats drink from communal bowls? No, because it's too easy for them to transfer germs to each other that way.

What about litter boxes? Again, it's best to have many around with different types of litter so cats can choose which box they like best. Otherwise, one or more of your cats may choose not to use any litter at all.

It seems like my cats are always sick. Is there anything I can do? It's very common for cats to pass illnesses back and forth, especially respiratory ones. Make sure you have good ventilation and lots of space for the cats, and wash your hands after petting a sick cat.

ONE OF MY CATS IS URINATING ALL OVER THE PLACE BUT I CAN'T FIGURE OUT WHICH ONE IS DOING IT. Your vet can inject a liquid called fluorescein which makes the suspect cat's urine visible under ultraviolet light, so you can know from the glow who's the culprit.

---

3 THINGS TO RUB ON YOUR CAT IF YOU OR SOMEONE CLOSE IS ALLERGIC

- A liquid product available in most pet stores and animal catalogues is Allerpet-C, which you rub on your cat to reduce the dander.

- A new saturated wipe that you rub on your cat reduces dander and saliva on its fur. Pals' Quick Cleansing Wipe from Pet Supplies Inc., PO Box 26211, Wauwatosa, WI 53226.

- Dust Seal, developed for people whose rugs and curtains make them sneeze, is said to work on cats and be harmless to them. Stir a tablespoon into a pint of water and sponge your cat with it.

How to Stop a Cat Fight and Protect Yourself

If your two cats get into a fight, you shouldn't step between them, and you shouldn't pick up either cat afterwards. "Cats should be left alone and never touched after a fight, as they can remain in an aroused state and attack any nearby living creature," says a Portland, Oregon feline behavior consultant, Renee Wrede.

When can you go near the cats again? "This arousal can last for minutes or even hours. Once the cat starts to groom himself, eat, or play, it's safe to be around him again," she says.

If you want to try to stop a fight *before* it starts, pay close attention to the cats' body language to see if the fight looks serious. If it does, shout "no" and see if that defuses matters. If it looks like it's escalating anyway, try making some kind of a sound at them. "I prefer 'PSSSST' to 'HSSSS' to get their attention," says Wrede. "A hiss can be too soft a sound and may not startle them enough. Sometimes a good 'SSHHHOOOO' while clapping your hands will startle them enough to make them run toward an escape route, such as an open door. Always offer an escape route."

Once a fight starts, some advocate using a broom to separate the cats or lift the paw of one cat off another. If you do so, be careful. "Some cats get so aroused they will fight with the broom and/or you," warns Wrede.

If the fighting cats are outdoors, you may be able to stop them by turning a hose on them or tossing a bucket of water at them.

OFFBEAT WAY TO STOP YOUR TWO CATS FROM FIGHTING

One woman with two cats kept classical music on for them all day and insisted it was the only thing that stopped them from fighting. Another cat owner who also reported that music diminished her cats' aggressiveness found that classical harp music works best.

IF YOUR FRIENDLY CATS
SUDDENLY HATE EACH OTHER

Two cats who were once close friends may suddenly dislike each other, especially after one returns from the vet. The sick cat may have picked up the smell of other cats or of the vet, reminding the remaining cat of unhappy times when he was there as well.

Dr. Michael Fox, author of *Supercat*, suggests that you dab a natural flower fragrance under the chins and around the backs and shoulders of both cats for a few days to mask the hated smells.

Do exercise caution. "It can be very dangerous to break up a cat fight. People can get serious—possibly life-threatening—infections from cat bites. The safest thing for you to do is walk away slowly, and when things are calm again, check kitty for injuries and visit the veterinarian if any are found," Ms. Wrede suggests.

INTRODUCING ANOTHER CAT INTO YOUR HOME

Before you actually bring a new cat into your house, it's good if your present pet has already smelled the new cat. Try to get the bedding of the new cat, or something that has been close to him, and bring it home, leaving it around your house for a couple of days so your cat gets used to the smell before the newcomer arrives.

Another way to make two cats familiar with each other's scent is to exchange litter boxes, but scoop out the solids before you switch them around.

Put a little perfume on both cats. They will trust each other more because their scents won't be strange to each other when they first meet.

And finally, if you want your two cats to get along, choose two cats from the same litter and it's more likely to happen.

18. Diseases You Can—and Can't—Catch from Your Cat

Diseases You Can Catch from Your Cat and How to Protect Yourself

You can—but probably won't—get a disease from your cat. If you do catch something, most of the thirty to fifty or so diseases can be easily cured and pose little long-term threat, except to the elderly and to immune-compromised people like those with AIDS.

Here are a few problems you ought to know about.

Ringworm is not a worm but more a fungus like athlete's foot. It can be transmitted by cats even when they don't show any symptoms. The spores are shed with their fur or transferred when they rub against the person, or when someone touches them.

Toxoplasmosis is a potentially very dangerous problem, but people are far more likely to catch it from raw meat than from a cat. Still, to play it safe, try to keep your cat from eating rodents

---

HOW LIKELY ARE YOU TO GET SICK FROM YOUR CAT?

Kay Lancaster, who treats cats and has spent a lifetime around them, says it all. "The total of diseases I've acquired is three infected cat bites and a few flea bites. Now, if you want to talk about the infections I've picked up from other people, well, there's measles, chicken pox, strep throat, innumerable colds, salmonella, shigella, a hundred or so cases of gastrointestinal whatsis, pneumonia, athlete's foot, a couple of bacterial skin infections.... Seems to me I'd be better off avoiding human society and just socializing with my critters.... Unfortunately, I happen to be very fond of my husband and family, with whom I've shared numerous contagious diseases."

and birds. Pregnant women must take extra-special precautions, since toxoplasmosis can cause birth defects. They must avoid contact with kitty litter or wear rubber gloves while handling the litter.

Ear mites can be transmitted from cat to human ears.

THE MAN WHO GAVE HIMSELF EAR MITES

Yes, someone really gave himself ear mites to prove that people could catch them from cats. But it's not a problem for the average person because he had to work hard to get the infection established, and then he didn't treat it.

It was indeed an unpleasant experience for him. He continually heard scratching and moving sounds in his ear and suffered from itching and pain. Eventually, it died down on its own.

For this sacrifice, he received not the Nobel Prize but the *Ig*noble Prize. Plus his "accomplishment" ended up in the veterinary textbooks—and in books like this as well.

The symptoms for ear mites in people are probably similar to the ones for cats: holding your head to one side, shaking it, scratching your ears, and finding dark specks in there. If you have these symptoms, check your cat.

Here are some things you can do to protect yourself and your children from zoonotic (animal-transmitted) diseases:

- Keeping cats free of fleas will probably help prevent many common and treatable problems, such as certain types of tapeworm—along with uncommon and not easily treated problems like the plague! So practice flea control.

- Flies, mosquitoes, and ticks are increasingly common carriers, so try to keep their populations down, and your cat out of heavily infested areas.

- A backyard can harbor dangerous organisms if your cat uses it as a litter box. Children, gardeners, and farmers touch the ground, which may be contaminated, and then they touch their faces and mouths, exposing themselves to diseases transmitted through urine and feces.

- If you have an outdoor cat, try to keep him out of parks where children play.
- Keep indoor litter boxes away from places where children can get to them, and always supervise their play areas.
- Make sure cat feces are disposed of properly, not just slightly buried.
- Don't let cats ingest stool.
- Keep your cat's nails trimmed.
- Wash your cat's feeding bowls and utensils separately from yours.
- Keep all vaccinations up-to-date.
- Report all unusual symptoms to your doctor.

Diseases You Can Give Your Cat

"Our ability to give cats diseases is not very high," says zoonotic (diseases man and animals share) expert Dr. James Miller. The common one would be strep, for we could be carriers and give it to our cats by breathing on them or coughing into a tissue which the cat then licks or ingests.

He said you can—but are extremely unlikely to—transmit the following to your cat:

Panleukopenia or feline distemper is a severe problem in cats. "We could be carriers of it—on our clothes or our hands— although people don't get this disease themselves."

IS CAT SCRATCH FEVER A TIGER OR A PUSSYCAT?

Some people are pretty nervous about this disease, but *USA Today* wrote that there were 22,000 reported cases of cat scratch fever in America each year and almost sixty million cats, making it a relatively rare problem.

Furthermore, you can also get cat scratch fever from dogs and other animals, who can transmit it even though they're not sick from it themselves. In fact, people have contracted it from non-living objects like plants or barbed wire.

Interestingly, one of the worst things that may happen to people who get this disease has nothing to do with cat scratch fever itself. Sometimes it's misdiagnosed as cancer of the lymph nodes!

Finally, there's no reason for someone who contracts a bad case to become nervous about keeping a sick cat in their house, because cats only have the disease for a short while. Once they give it to someone, they probably won't give it to them again later.

If you get a bad scratch, wash it with soap and water and put an antibiotic ointment on it. If the scratch is very bad, or doesn't improve immediately, go to a doctor for stronger treatment.

Lyme disease: A tick only attaches and transfers the bacterium once in each cycle, so a tick can't attach itself to you, give you Lyme disease, fall off, and then give your cat the disease too.

"However, a tick could dislodge from you before it has completely attached itself, or get on your clothes and fall off without ever attaching itself to you, and then attach itself to your cat," says Miller. If your cat doesn't then dislodge it by grooming, "your" infected tick could give him Lyme disease.

Why You Can't Catch AIDS from Cats with FIV

Cats get FIV (Feline Immunodeficiency Virus), the feline equivalent of the virus that causes AIDS in humans. Although FIV resembles HIV—both are lentiviruses—FIV can't be transmitted to humans, nor can cats get HIV from people.

FIV cats should be kept away from other cats since they can infect each other through bites or scratches. Kittens of infected mothers can also be born with FIV. You should also have any new cats brought into your house tested for the virus—twice.

The FIV virus has infected twenty-five species of cats throughout the world, but the reason we don't have to worry about it is that there's a long list of things FIV (or HIV) must do to infect the host. These were outlined in *Discovery* magazine, which said that first the virus has to find the right cell in the host animal. Then it must infect that cell, take over the cellular machinery, make a copy of itself, release that copy, escape the host's immune surveillance, and then infect another cell.

"It's a lockstep process, and if at any point the virus makes a mistake, the host will almost certainly kill it. Thus FIV seldom infects a new, even close related, species," writes Virginia Morell. And we are not closely related to cats, so it certainly won't affect people.

The plague: The most virulent form, pneuomonic plague, is passed by respiratory secretions, so if you have the plague (heaven help you!) it would be possible for you to give it to your cat just by breathing on him or coughing into a tissue which he then licks or ingests. "But it would have to be the early stages because later, you would be so sick, you would be in the hospital and not home with your cat," says Miller.

SHOULD PEOPLE WITH AIDS KEEP THEIR CATS?

Yes, say experts, who cite a 1993 study showing a decrease in depressive symptoms among HIV-infected people who own pets. Still, anyone with immune-system problems should be aware that they are more susceptible to zoonotic diseases, and some diseases like cat scratch fever and toxoplasmosis can be more troublesome to those whose resistance is low.

But the benefits of having a cat or any beloved pet—especially at a time in the person's life when they need extra comfort and closeness—surely outweigh the risks. And if there are problems caring for pets, there are wonderful people who will help them.

There are two humanitarian groups available to help people with AIDS who have pets. They are PAWS (Pets Are Wonderful Support) and POWARS (Pet Owners with AIDS Resource Service). Some of the volunteers will take pets of people who can't care for them, bring food to those who can't get out, or come to their houses and do everything right down to changing litter boxes if necessary.

Do Cats Get Herpes—
and Can They Give It to You?

Herpes in cats, unless the victim is a kitten—in which case it can be fatal—is generally quite mild, with symptoms similar to a cold or an upper respiratory infection. Symptoms include sneezing, swollen stuffy nose, and inflamed eyes. After treatment, the disease becomes dormant, but may show up again later under stress.

Herpes is contagious among cats, and when people hear the words "contagious" or "herpes," they become frightened. "But it's an extremely species-specific disease among cats, so they can't give it to you," says Dr. James Miller, a zoonotic expert from the University of Prince Edward Island.

"Humans generally get herpes type one or two on the lips and the genitals, respectively. Neither of these kind can be given to our cats, and the kind they have can't be given to us," he assured us.

Can Your Cat Get Mad Cat Disease?

The chances of your cat getting mad cow diseases (bovine spongiform encephalopathy or BSE) are almost infinitesimal, even if you live in England. Although it's true a few cats did get it there, and in Holland also, there's still no cause for concern.

The disease, which can be spread by consumption of brains and spinal cords of infected animals, may have been transmitted to pets through their food, which contained the remains of cows with mad cow disease. But the United States has been very watchful about this, and has not imported processed beef or cattle from England in almost ten years. In addition, America uses a higher heat for the rendering processes, which would deactivate the protein.

The bottom line: Don't worry anywhere, now. The few cats who got BSE were mostly cats in the Netherlands who ate a British cat food made with diseased beef, and the food was never sold in the United States.

Can You Give Your Cats a Cold— and Can You Catch Theirs?

You won't catch a cold directly from a sick cat, since most of the organisms that infect a cat's nose and throat have no effect on people. And you won't give your cat your cold directly for similar reasons.

But if you *touch* a cat who has a cold, and then you touch your cat, you can spread that cat's respiratory infection to your own cat if you didn't wash your hands after handling the sick one.

Your cat can also catch that other cat's cold without your intervention. Cats can give each other colds directly, and in fact, a cold is the most likely illness for cats to catch from one another. Fortunately, it's not one of the more serious ones, so the cold is mostly just much a-choo about nothing.

19. How to Help Your Cat Live Longer

Have an Older Cat? New Pill May Make Old Cats Act "Young" Again

Is your old cat acting differently? Perhaps he can't find the litter box, he's howling at night, or he's acting as if he's lost when he's right in your own house. Your cat could be showing the signs of senility—but a drug that has worked wonders in this area with dogs shows great promise for cats as well.

The drug is called 1-deprenyl, and was recently given FDA approval for limited use in dogs. "I've received some calls from veterinarians who are treating old cats who are missing the litter box when they had no trouble hitting it for fifteen years," says Dr. Bill Ruehl, VP of Scientific Affairs for Deprenyl Animal Health in Overland Park, Kansas.

Another problem of older cats is what is called inappropriate vocalization. "The cat may be howling at night and sometimes during the day with no reason for it, such as another cat outside."

Other symptoms owners of older cats have complained about are that "sometimes the cats seem to get lost in their home. Or they become spacey and don't recognize their owners."

Did deprenyl work for cats as well as it works for dogs? "I've received reports from veterinarians who have given it to fifteen to twenty cats, and some have had a good response to it. They have not reported any problems with safety either," said Ruehl.

So if your cat is acting its age, ask your vet about this pill. It's not the Fountain of Youth, but if it works, it's a lot better than living with the alternatives.

Why Cats Live Longer Than They Used to Live

It has been said that the only fault of cats is that their lives are too short. At about seven a cat can be considered middle-aged, and around nine to ten or more they're geriatric. Outdoor cats may only live to five to ten years, feral cats only one to two years, and an indoor cat should live to around sixteen or seventeen.

But fifty years ago cats rarely made it to ten and were more likely to die by eight or sooner. Why? Cats used to be utilitarian creatures, kept around to catch rodents and cared for only to the extent that they were useful.

Guy Hodge, director of data and information for the Humane Society of the United States, said that animals "weren't taken to veterinarians, there were no diagnostic tests, and few treatments

---

HOW OLD IS YOUR CAT IN PEOPLE YEARS?

We tried not to include in this book things you find in lots of other cat books, and the following chart does appear frequently, but it's something people want to see often, so here it is.

When your cat is ...

6 months old, it's the equivalent of a person 7$^1/_2$ to 10 years old

1 year = 15 to 20 years	8 = 48	16 = 80
2 = 24	9 = 52	17 = 84
3 = 28	10 = 56	18 = 88
4 = 32	11 = 60	19 = 90
5 = 36	12 = 64	20 = 96
6 = 40	13 = 68	21 = 100
7 = 44	14 = 72	
	15 = 76	

---

for cure or prevention. There was no neutering, which tends to extend the animal's life expectancy by protecting the animal from certain types of cancers, and reduces the male's inclination to roam, when he may get lost or hit by a car."

Cats were also kept outside and not fed very well. "There was no good quality pet food—they were fed the scraps. Most of the money used to be put into advertising, and they put out a cheaper product. Also, today's food causes fewer difficulties, like stomach problems and diabetes."

Improved flea control is also a factor. "They used to get rid of fleas by putting strong compounds on animals, like DDT," Hodge said.

Today, hearing aids are being developed to correct deafness, and there is cataract surgery to restore sight, hip replacement, chemotherapy and radiation treatment, cardiac ultrasound, ECG, and MRIs for cats and dogs. In the next decade, cats will live even longer.

Help Your Older Cat Live to 25 (Okay, 20)

More than 10 percent of all pet cats in America are over eleven; here are ways you may help your older cat double that.

FOOD AND WATER:

- Watch how much they drink, since kidneys are often the first organ to deteriorate. If they're drinking less, put a little water on your finger and dab it on the side of their mouths, or put a little in their food. If they're drinking more, take them to a vet.
- Feed them smaller meals without reducing the overall amount of food.
- Switch to a seniors diet.

REDUCING STRESS:

- Talk louder, since an older cat's hearing is not as acute as that of younger cats.
- Since they may not hear or see as well as they used to, keep things calm and consistent.
- Lift them up or buy or build a little ramp to help them get up and down from high places since they can't jump as well as they used to.
- Let them sleep more without disturbance.
- Let them be alone more if they wish.

MORE FREQUENT VET VISITS:

- If their behavior or appearance changes, take them to a vet, especially if they seem to have arthritis, stomach, or teeth problems.
- Take them to the vet for checkups more often anyway since more is likely to go wrong as they get older, and they're less physically able to cope with it.

THE MAIN REASONS CATS END UP IN HOSPITALS

Mike Capuzzo, pet writer in *Newsday* and author of a delightful book called *Wild Things*, listed the main reasons cats wind up in the hospital:

- Fan-belt injuries (from cats napping in car engines)
- Hairballs in long-haired and infrequently groomed cats
- Twists and sprains from claws getting caught on drapes and fabrics
- Cancer, leukemia, and lymphoma
- Feline urological syndrome
- Dental problems (mouth bleeding, missing teeth, bad breath)

Cat Constipation and Diarrhea: How to Prevent and Treat Them

CONSTIPATION TREATMENT:

- a small amount of canned pumpkin or strained prunes mixed in with a cat's dry food relieves constipation
- mineral oil
- a little petroleum jelly, or Petromalt, malt-flavored petroleum jelly, rubbed into their paw so they lick it off also helps

CONSTIPATION PREVENTION:

- soluble fiber in the diet
- commercial products to prevent furballs
- a little butter or Vaseline in their food a couple of times a week can help with constipation
- regular grooming to remove hair from their coat is important since hairballs can cause potentially deadly constipation
- keep the litter box clean so your cats are comfortable using it
- don't change litter brands suddenly, or they may stop defecating long enough to cause problems

DIARRHEA TREATMENT:

- cooked rice in the food
- low-fat yogurt
- lactobacillus milk
- a bland diet like chicken or baby food for a day or two will help with diarrhea.

If either condition persists past that, see a vet.

20. How to Save Your Cat's Life and Keep Her from Danger

71 Ways You Can Help Save Your Cat's Life

Cats and kittens have been impaled by high-heeled shoes. Plastic bags from the cleaners have suffocated untold numbers of pets. And that's just for starters. Sadly, most people don't know about the common hazards that face—and often kill—cats daily. But many freak accidents could be prevented if the owners were aware there was a danger. Here are some little-known hazards and how to minimize them.

In the Kitchen:

- Keep **bones** secure and out of the reach of your cat.
- Hide **twine or cord** used to truss poultry or meat to prevent intestinal blockage.
- **Pot handles** for pans holding hot liquids on the stove should be pointed inward.
- **Plastic rings from six-packs** should be disposed of safely. Snip the rings so they can't strangle your cat.
- Place your **refrigerator** as close to the wall as possible so your cat can't get behind it.
- Never leave **moist cat food** out longer than fifteen minutes. Discard what's uneaten.
- **Counters, shelves, and cupboards** must be wiped clean, especially if you use insecticides.
- When **cleaning or waxing** kitchen floors, put your cat elsewhere until floors dry. Cats can absorb dangerous products through their foot pads.
- Close **oven and cabinet doors** so cats can't be locked in accidentally.

- Wrap **harmful leftovers** in a separate bag before placing them in the garbage.
- Secure all **trash containers,** indoors and out.
- Consider **burner covers** for your stove, especially if you have pilot lights.
- Don't close your **refrigerator** door until you've checked for your cat inside.
- Don't use **aerosol sprays** near a cat's food or water bowl.
- Keep **chemicals and cleaners** in a closed cabinet.

IN THE BATHROOM AND LAUNDRY:

- **Pills** should be kept sealed in their containers in a closed medicine cabinet.
- **Toilet lids** should be kept down.
- **Talcum powder** cans should be closed so the talc can't be inhaled.
- Never give **human drugs** to a cat unless instructed by your vet.
- Unplug **appliances** like electric toothbrushes and dryers if your kitten's teething.

IS ASPIRIN SAFE FOR CATS?

It depends on what kind and the dosage. Regular aspirin must be given in small doses at long intervals since it takes two days for felines to metabolize aspirin. Don't try to come up with the proper dosages yourself. For example, a 10-pound cat does not get $1/10$ of the dose of a 100-pound human. The amount and timing of the doses are different.

Ibuprofin (Advil, Motrin) is another matter and can make your cat very sick. Acetaminophen pills—for example Tylenol—are even worse. Just one dose can kill a cat. If you see a purplish tinge to your cat's gums and he has difficulty breathing, he could have ingested a fatal amount of Tylenol.

- Always unplug **irons** and put away **ironing boards.**
- Never start a **washing machine or dryer** or close a **dresser drawer** until you've made sure your cat is not inside.

IN OTHER ROOMS

- **Pennies** minted after 1982 contain 96 percent zinc, which is poisonous.
- **Golf balls** may have toxic liquid centers.
- **Lamp cords** should be sprayed with cat-repellent material and should be disconnected.
- **Plastic garment bags** from dry cleaners should be discarded carefully.
- **Window screens** should be locked securely, and windows closed to prevent cats from falling out.
- **Water in flower vases** may be toxic from the flowers.
- Easily swallowed **small toys** should be kept out of harm's way.
- Don't let your cat sleep too long in front of a **fireplace or space heater or on a heating pad.**

A BIG DANGER TO KITTENS—AND YOU

One of the biggest dangers in your house is electrical cords, which are very popular with teething kittens. They like to chew on them, and occasionally bite through, presenting a serious hazard to themselves, and to you if you attempt to disconnect your cat from the cord.

Don't touch a cat with a wire in his mouth, or you can get shocked yourself. Disconnect the cord first, or move the cat away from the cord with a nonconducting object like a wooden cane or broom.

Also, don't treat this as a minor problem afterwards. Even if his burn seems minor, consult your vet immediately since electric shock can lead to sudden death a few hours later.

THE DRYER CAN BE DIRE FOR YOUR CAT

A clothes dryer can be one of the most dangerous things in your house for a cat, says Gina Spadafori, who writes an interesting column called *Pet Connection* that appears weekly in the Pet Care Forum on America Online.

This pet expert, who knows of three cats who have died in dryers, explains that the cat crawls into the dryer to sleep, attracted by the warm clothes. Someone adds a few more items, or thinks the ones in there need a bit more drying. "Like a dog in a hot car, this is a horrible way to die," she says.

- Keep **looped cords from blinds and drapes** out of reach.
- **Candles** shouldn't be burned in accessible spots or when untended.
- Turn **halogen lamps** off when no one's around to prevent fires, since cats can knock lamps down.
- Extinguish all **cigarettes and other smoking materials** and keep them away from your cat.
- **Tools and household wares** like glue, cellophane tape, rubber bands, nails, thumbtacks, etc., are all potentially dangerous items.

ON THE GROUNDS:

- **Insecticides or herbicides** can be poisonous. Keep your cat away from a freshly treated lawn or garden. Water your lawn to help chemicals sink in, and wait twenty-four hours before allowing your cat into the area.
- **Potting soil** may be chemically treated and could be poisonous.
- **Garbage containers** should be sealed with tight, secure lids, to stop your cat from eating rotten food.
- **Poisonous insects, snakes, and scorpions** are potential dangers.

- **Wild animals,** such as skunks, rats, raccoons, possums, wood-chucks, toads, rabbits, and bats, can poison or infect your cat with rabies and tick-borne diseases.
- **Rat poison** doesn't only kill rats.
- Outside **water supplies** should be pure and free from icing up.
- Even clean-looking water can be contaminated by **animals, chemicals, or blue-green algae.**
- **Semi-frozen ponds and puddles** pose a terrible winter threat to your cat—and to an owner who goes out in the ice to try to bring a cat in.
- **Sharp objects,** natural and otherwise, could be a danger to your cat, from fishhooks to porcupine quills, cactus, and thistles.
- **Balconies and terraces** should be off-limits for cats; they don't always land feet-first. Indoor cats haven't learned to judge distances and heights the way outdoor cats can.
- **Salt spread on roadways and sidewalks** to help keep them clear of ice and snow can be ingested orally and through paw pads.
- **Fences** can be missing boards or have spaces at the bottom.
- Avoid **frostbite** in your cat by immediately removing snow and ice from your cat's face and body.

In the Garage and the Car:

- Keep cats in **crates** when driving in a car. Cats are dangerously erratic. Keep air conditioning on in warm weather.
- Never put the crate with the cat inside in the **trunk.** (This would seem obvious, yet people do it.)
- Even if the car is just in the garage, **brake fluid, carburetor cleaner, and gasoline** are potentially lethal.
- **Antifreeze** causes thousands of pet deaths each year. Puddles of antifreeze under parked cars in garages and on the street can cause fatal injury. There is antifreeze that is safe for pets.

- **Window-washer solution** contains antifreeze.
- Before starting your car, **bang on the hood** or **tap your horn a few times** in case your cat has picked your warm engine as a place to nap.

OTHER HAZARDS:

- **Flea dips** can poison cats that have skin problems or open sores.
- Some cats have a low tolerance to **flea collars.**
- Brush excess **flea powder** off your cat thirty minutes after application.
- **Collars and muzzles** can cause problems or death by strangulation. Make sure you know how to use them, and watch out they don't get caught on the insides of kennels or crates.
- **Elizabethan-style cone-shaped oversized collars** which cats occasionally wear for medical reasons can lead to freak accidents.

Cats Need Sunscreen, Too!

Cats—especially short-haired, light-colored, and short-groomed ones—can have problems because of the sun. This includes skin cancer, generally appearing on their ears and nose, which may then have to be surgically removed. Poor kitty!

There is a company that makes pet sunscreen, and they say it's a good idea to put some blocker on your cat, especially on the nose and ears where cats can't lick it off.

This shouldn't only be done on outdoor cats. If your cat spends a lot of time in the sun, even if it's only by a sunny window indoors, use sunscreen.

A more common problem than skin cancer is sunstroke or heat stroke if your cat is exposed to too much sun or heat. It doesn't take long for this to happen, so watch for symptoms like listlessness, labored breathing, and, sometimes, frothing at the mouth.

If you see this happening—or if you see your cat start to pant—do something immediately. Dip him in cool water, or wrap him in wet towels while rushing him to the vet. But don't keep dunking him in water since rapid temperature swings can also be dangerous.

The Number One Enemy of Cats

It's not other animals.

It's not humans.

It's cars. Dr. Bruce Fogle, author of *101 Questions Your Cat Would Ask Its Vet If It Could Talk,* points out that nothing in cats' evolution prepares them for cars, and headlights cause them to freeze.

The solution? Reflective collars. And keeping your cat indoors. After all, he's less likely to be hit by a car in your house than in the street.

---

2 WAYS TO TELL IF YOUR CAT IS
DANGEROUSLY DEHYDRATED

Dehydration is a perilous side effect of fever. Here's a simple test recommended by *Cats* magazine.

Lift the skin at the scruff of his neck and hold it for thirty seconds. When you release the scruff, it should flatten to normal in less than a second. If it takes five seconds or more to flatten out, call the vet.

Also, you can test for dehydration and low blood pressure by pressing your finger against the cat's gums. The spot should turn white right away. If it takes more than two seconds to return to pink, there's a problem.

Here are some ways to prevent some sun- and heat-related difficulties.

- If your cat is a likely candidate for skin cancer, and you see a sore on his ears, nose, or eyes, don't assume it's from a cat fight. If it hasn't gotten better in a week, see a vet.
- Don't leave cats to swelter without shelter. Keep them indoors if it's really hot, or try to provide something for them outside with a roof over it.
- If you leave a cat indoors when you go to work, leave the air conditioning on.
- Make sure there's plenty of fresh water available.
- Never keep a cat inside a car when it's hot outside. The sun may not be on the car when you leave, but it can shift quickly. Furthermore, you may think you're only going to spend a few minutes where you are, but you may bump into a friend, get delayed in a line, or forget about your cat and wander off.

How to Use the Heimlich Maneuver to Save Your Cat's Life

If your cat is choking, you can do a modified version of the Heimlich maneuver. But since it carries risks to your cat, even before you try it, you should open his mouth to look for the stuck object. Obviously, the following is better done with two people:

- Place one hand on your cat's upper jaw with your thumb on one side, and the rest of your fingers on the other.
- With your other hand, push down on the lower jaw, keeping your index finger free to sweep back into his mouth.
- If you can see or feel the object, remove it. If it's not easily removed, use long-nosed pliers if some are nearby.

If you can't see the object, and you know something's there, use a modified Heimlich for a cat, explained by Warren Eckstein in *How to Get Your Cat to Do What You Want.*

- Place your cat on his side on a hard surface.
- Locate his last rib, and place both your hands behind it.
- Press down, firmly and quickly, moving your hands slightly forward as you do it.
- Keep doing it until the object pops out.

Vaccinations Can Give Cats Cancer

Veterinarians throughout the country are noticing a new and frightening phenomenon: Cats being given vaccines like the ones for feline leukemia and rabies are very occasionally getting a deadly form of cancer at the injection site.

Dr. Mike Richards, co-owner of Mathews Veterinary Services in Cobbs Creek, Virginia, explains why this is happening: "About ten years ago, they changed animal vaccines from a modified live virus to a killed one, thinking it was safer. But for a killed virus to work it must have a powerful adjuvent which is irritating to the immune system."

The result, he explained, is that a small number of cats "will develop a cancer at the injection site. It's a really aggressive tumor that kills 50 percent of them."

Why are cats given the injection then? "Actually, it's causing vets to rethink the situation," he said. "With feline leukemia, for example, right now vets are saying 'I'll vaccinate the cat even if he's an

---

SPOTTING THE SIGNS OF CANCER IN YOUR CAT

"There are many different types of cancer, each with its own symptoms," says one of the top cat/dog surgeons in the country, Dr. Richard Greene of the Manhattan Veterinary Group Ltd. in New York City.

"Some of the symptoms include: weight loss (for example, in leukemia); tumors (such as mammary tumors); lumps or growths that don't heal or keep on growing and enlarge; bloody urine (for bladder tumors); abdominal distention and skin and gums turning yellow (liver cancer); coughing, labored breathing, or shortness of breath (lung cancer); weakness or depression."

He added that "tumors becoming malignant in cats is a common situation, so any tumors should immediately be shown to a veterinarian. And you should see your vet for any of the symptoms I mentioned."

---

inside cat and has no risk in case he gets out.' But because of this cancer, some are starting to think that maybe they shouldn't.

"With rabies, veterinarians don't have much of a choice about giving the injections because the law demands that cats be given them. And if a cat bites someone and doesn't have a current injection, the cat may have to be put to sleep."

The American Veterinary Medical Association is currently studying the problem of these injection-induced cancers. Meanwhile you should probably go ahead and let your cat have the necessary shots because the cancer is less common than the diseases he might get without them.

Here are some vaccination tips that could save your cat, offered by Dr. Amy Marder, a well-known veterinarian and pet author:

1. Avoid unnecessary vaccinations, like the feline leukemia virus, if your cat doesn't go outside or come into contact with other cats.

2. Make a note of where your vet is giving a shot since the chance of cancer increases if the injections are given at the same site.

3. Feel for bumps where your vet administered the vaccination. Fibrosarcoma can show up from three months to three years after vaccination.

4. Ask your vet not to vaccinate between the shoulder blades because that's a difficult place to remove a tumor later if one should arise.

5. Ask for a modified live virus if you can get it.

Earthquakes (Listen Up, California Cats)

If you live in an area prone to tremors, you know how upsetting even minor quakes are for your cats. The television show *The Pet Channel* gave the following suggestions to which West Coast cat owners will want to pay special attention:

- Know your cat's favorite hiding places—that's where he's likely to head, even before the quake itself.
- During and after a quake, hold and caress your cat.
- Cat owners should always have a hard, plastic carrier near at hand.

HOW TO MAKE AN OUTDOOR CAT AN INDOOR ONE

Can't decide whether to make the switch? Remember that your cat is asleep most of the time anyway. And where would he sleep the best? Some place warm in the winter and cool in the summer and safe all year round. Or in the freezing cold or debilitating heat, perhaps under a car?

Furthermore, there are all kinds of advantages to being an indoor cat. The most important is that it adds several years to his life—it may even double his life expectancy—since it reduces the risk of his being hit or hurt by cars, dogs, troublemakers, or other cats.

How do you make the switch?

- Make or buy a window perch so he can continue to look outside.
- Give him something to watch outside that he would enjoy, for example, a birdhouse in his view.
- Mix a little outdoor dirt or sand in with his kitty litter and change over gradually.
- Buy a container of premixed grass in a little pot and let him munch on that.

- A supply of bottled water and canned food should be available.
- Know where medication, blankets, and a first aid book are (and they should be easy to find).
- All cats should have a means of identification that won't be lost. Tattoos or microchip ID's, in addition to tags on collars, should be considered.
- Keep prepared during the aftershock periods, which last several days after a quake.

EXPERIMENTS ON CATS BY STUDENTS

Between five and six million animals in America—including cats—are used in experiments each year, some by junior high and high school students, according to the ASPCA. Chillingly, there is no law limiting what a researcher may do to an animal as part of an experiment.

The ASPCA writes that high school students "may be encouraged to do animal-based science projects ... often involv[ing] administration of painful stimuli or noxious substances, or even surgery of animals.... Unlike biomedical research experiments, whose purpose is to gather new data, most educational projects are nothing more than repetitive exercises ... performed by students who are untrained in surgical techniques ... caus[ing] pain and stress to countless animals, yet providing no new or useful information." Incidentally, computer graphic dissection can now replace much of this.

10 Products You Can Buy That Could Save Your Cat's Life

Pet Rescue Decals: They alert firemen and rescue workers to cats in your home. Free with ten proofs of purchase of 9-Lives Plus canned pet food, plus fifty cents postage and handling, and your name and address on a three-by-five-inch postcard to 9-Lives Pet Rescue Offer, Dept. OF, P.O. Box 8026, Young America, MN 55551-8026.

First Aid for Pets Kits: Kits with emergency supplies, such as bandages and tools to treat injuries, bites, cuts, wounds, burns, and eye problems, are distributed by Pet-Pak, Inc. Call toll free at 1-800-217-PETS.

Animal Life Vests: Brightly colored vests with reflective tape are a must for you cat's next boating trip. Vests cost $45 and $55, depending on size, plus shipping and handling. Call 707-939-3788.

Blinking Outdoor Collars: A blinking red light on your cat's collar makes your pet visible at night to oncoming drivers. $7 or $8 for one with automatic light sensor. Add $3.50 s/h. Call Protect-A-Pet, Inc., at 1-800-835-9899.

Non-tipping Cat Window Shelf: A padded platform that fits most window sills gives your cat a safe indoor spot. $30 + $5.50 s/h. Call Hobar Co. at 508-829-3144.

Pet Doors: Help your outdoor cat make a successful dash into the house when he's being chased by a dog! These self-closing, lockable, and weatherproof devices are available from Petdoors USA. From $19 to $356. 1-800-749-9609.

Make Garage Doors Safe: Eliminate deadly accidents caused by curious cats who check out the space above open garage doors. The prices are $49.95 and $89.95 for a safety curtain for one- and two-door garages. Feline Safety Curtain, Box 2692, Bellaire, TX 77402 or call at 713-271-8414.

K-9 Carts: Paralyzed cats don't have to be put to sleep. K-9 carts can give them mobility indoors and out. From $205 to $220. Call 406-995-3111.

Ramp for Elderly Cats: Your cat could break a leg trying to jump when he no longer can. The PawsWay Ramp, from Pet Care with Love, is placed next to a bed, couch, or chair and lets your older animal have easy access to their favorite places. $70 / $97 / $140. Call 1-800-441-1765.

Cat Sunscreen: Cats can get skin cancer, so you might want to apply this SPF15 spray, which also keeps bugs away. SunSpot, $8.99 + $3.00 s/h. Call 617-242-9282.

COULD YOUR CAT SAVE YOUR CHILD'S LIFE?

Could your cat be a canary? Canaries alert coal miners to gases, and cats may alert house owners to lead in time to save their children.

Children can have lead poisoning even without having external signs, but cats do get symptoms that can tip people off. In one case a cat had clear signs of lead intoxication (vomiting, weight loss, sleeplessness, and seizures), resulting in the children in the home being tested. The children were given treatment in time to rid their bodies of lead—and so was the cat.

Should You Keep a Handicapped Cat?

If your pet has become handicapped, you may have to make some changes.

If it's happening gradually, it isn't as much of a problem as when it happens suddenly, because the cat has time to compensate for the loss of one sense with his others. For example, blind cats will become more aware of auditory cues, and deaf cats may become extra sensitive to vibrations in their environment.

Here are a few things you can do to help them in their adjustments, whether their problems happened slowly or suddenly.

Blindness: Don't change the furniture, food, or water bowls around.

Deafness: Don't let him go outside, where there are dangers he can't hear, like cars.

Also, try not to startle him when you approach.him. Since he generally responds to vibrations, knock on something next to him so he feels the vibration before you arrive.

By the way, always consider the possibility of deafness when you buy a white kitten; check his hearing carefully.

Lameness: If he's too arthritic to get up and down from elevated places, get a ramp that enables him to climb up where he once leaped. And do him a favor and keep him inside for the winter.

Paralysis: Look into those little carts that attach to pets' legs and enable paralyzed cats to wheel around.

Keeping Your Cat from Plants and Soil

What do you do if your cat likes your plants as much as you do? Here are some suggestions given to us by Joel Rapp—known as Mr. Mother Earth—on how to keep cats away from plants, and stop them from digging up the dirt around them.

OUTDOOR PLANTS:

- Grow catnip near your cat's favorite plant so he goes after that instead. Catnip may also repel insects, so that's another good reason to plant it.
- Grow rue plants, which are malodorous enough to discourage cats from nibbling at your garden.

PESTICIDE-FREE GARDENING

If you have a cat who goes outdoors, you don't want to use pesticides in your garden. Here are a few suggestions from the Project BREED Rescue Directory on humane gardening, and the science section of the *New York Times* on what plants can be used as alternatives to pesticides.

- Marigold will repel beetles.
- Mice dislike daffodil bulbs and garlic plants, and it's more humane to keep mice away using plants than to let your cat dispose of the mice.
- Flies and mosquitoes are diminished by planting basil.
- Spearmint helps get rid of ants from your porch, patio, or deck.
- Chrysanthemums, patchouli, vetiver, citronella, peppermint, and pennyroyal may also repel insects without using pesticides.
- Also osage orange may scare off insects, or the latex in the leaves may interfere with their mouth parts.

INDOOR PLANTS:

- Keep the soil moist since cats like to dig in dry places.
- Put decorative rocks on top of the dirt.
- Mix some green vegetables in with your cat's food.
- Buy your cat his own plant of grass blades or catnip, so he'll favor it.
- Hang the plants too high for him to reach.
- Put a thin layer of pebbles over the soil around your plants, which takes away some of the soil smell that attracts your cat and may make him urinate in the soil.
- To keep him from eating the plants, you can also put substances that he doesn't like on the leaves.
- Finally, if your cat eats a poisonous plant, call your vet, or the National Animal Poison Control Center (1-800-548-2423) located at the College of Veterinary Medicine at the University of Illinois. The price is $30 per case. If you don't have a credit card, call 1-900-680-0000. The cost of the call is $20 for five minutes and $2.95 each additional minute. Have the following information ready when you call: your name, address, phone number; species, breed, age, sex, and weight of your cat; the poison you believe he has ingested; and the problems he is experiencing.

21. These Are Dirty Jobs But You've Gotta Do Them

How to Give Your Cat Pills or Eye Medication

Even before you start medicating your cat:

- Store the pills or capsules in a closed container filled with her favorite treats. The medicinal smell will be reduced, and the pills will absorb a flavor she likes.
- Choose the bathroom or a small room for the treatment, so you don't have to chase your cat all over the house if she bolts. You might also try wrapping her in a towel or using a commercial restrainer that only leaves the face free.
- Have everything ready in advance, so you don't have to set things up while you're holding her down. If you're wrapping her in a towel, grab the towel first and not the cat first so you'll be ready when your cat is.
- Wear heavy gloves, if possible.
- Try to work with two people (minimum).
- Always check the label with any medication to see if refrigeration is required.

GIVING PILLS

- A pill gun can be very helpful.
- You can also try hiding the pill in a favorite treat—but make sure your cat's not hiding the pill in her mouth (unswallowed) afterwards.
- The best way to hide the pill is to pulverize it manually or with a pill crusher and put it in something like butter or cream cheese. Then, put the butter on your cat's paws so she'll lick it off. But check with your vet first, because not all pills should be broken down or mixed with other items.

Liquid Medication: Easier Ways to Get It Down

- Saturate a small piece of bread with the liquid medication and put it in your cat's mouth. The bread is easy for her to swallow and the liquid medicine won't spill. Check with your vet to ensure that it is okay to give that particular medicine in that manner.

- It's also been suggested that you spill the liquid medicine on your cat's fur—and she will then lap it up. Either that, or she'll be sticky for a long time, and so will you after you touch her.

- If you're trying to give the medication to her directly, use a long-handled spoon, preferably larger than the amount of liquid you have to put in it so it's harder for the medicine to spill out.

- Give her the medicine slowly, so she doesn't inhale it.

- Dress appropriately so you don't ruin evening wear with splashed-on cat medication.

- It helps to wet capsules with water or coat them with a little butter or margarine to make them go down better. (Again, check with your vet first, because this shouldn't be done on all capsules.) Don't wet pills, though. If they start to dissolve before they get in your cat's mouth, they may taste even worse to him.

- Place the pill or capsule as far back in your cat's mouth as you can, and then quickly remove your hand from her mouth. Cover the nostrils with a finger or hold her head up and stroke her throat, which makes a cat swallow.

Eye Medication

Liquid:

- If you're using a dropper, hold up your cat's upper eyelid and put the medication inside the top of the eye. Close her eyelids together and rub gently. Wait about fifteen seconds so the drops don't fall out.

Ointment:

- Don't let the applicator touch your cat's eye, which can contaminate the medication.

- With clean hands, apply a small amount to one finger. Then, pull down your cat's lower eyelid slightly, put a dab right inside the rim, close her eyelids together, and rub gently. Using your finger will prevent the tube from poking her in the eye, and makes applying it easier.

Taking Your Cat's Temperature

Touching the tips of a cat's ears will sometimes tell you if a cat has a fever, but that's not a very scientific method.

Still, it's understandable that one would try to avoid actually having to take a cat's temperature, since it should take at least two people to hold a cat firmly, and three if your cat's hind legs need to be held down, too.

However many people you have, here goes. Lubricate a special pet thermometer with K-Y or mineral oil first. Gently lift your cat's tail up. Insert the thermometer about an inch into the rectum, and point it slightly upwards as you put it in.

Leave it there for about two minutes while talking to your cat in a soothing voice. Never let go of his legs!

A normal temperature is 100.5 to 102.5 degrees. Yours may rise to that, too.

Should You Bathe Your Cat—and What If Fluffy Gets Dandruff-y?

Bathing a cat has been described as martial art, so it should be a relief that experts say you generally don't have to do it. "Cats shouldn't be bathed unless they get into something or get fleas or some other condition," says Dr. Margaret Muns, staff veterinarian

---

THESE TIPS WILL HELP YOU BATHE YOUR CAT

- Put a rubber mat or towel at the bottom of the sink or tub to give your cat something to hold onto is a suggestion from *The Complete Idiot's Guide to Living with a Cat,* by Carolyn Janik and Ruth Rejnis.
- Only use a few inches of warm water and special cat shampoo.
- A new gadget called Bathe'N Carry seems terrific except for the price. It looks a little like an enlarged slinky. It fits over your cat, containing wide enough spaces between the wires so that you can wash through the hoops without major trauma. Bathe'N'Carry: $39.95, Prima International, 18525 East Gale Avenue, City of Industry, CA 91748, 1-800-446-5696.

---

at CompuServe's TW Pet forum. "I wouldn't put both of you through the stress of bathing for the occasional dandruff/oil spots, which are not unusual in the winter when the furnace is on."

As for dandruff, which can come from poor quality food, dry skin, illness, or just plain old age, to get rid of it:

- Use special shampoo.
- Brush your cat more frequently.
- Run a humidifier in your house.
- Give your cat better food.

If these simple remedies don't work, or the pet's coat gets worse, consult your veterinarian.

How to Keep Your Cat from Having a Bad Hair Day

Most owners are so glad when they're finally finished bathing their reluctant-to-be-washed cat that they breathe a sigh of relief when the ordeal is over and let their cats dash off to dry naturally. That's why cats often look so scruffy and matted after their baths.

It's better to use a blow dryer (set on low) on your cat before setting her free—that is, if both of you have the strength to continue after the bath.

Brushing Up On Your Cat's Teeth

What's the number one diagnosed disease of cats that go to a vet? Oral disease. According to a University of Minnesota study, 70 percent of felines show signs of gum disease by the time they're three years old—and a lot of it could have been prevented if people had only brushed and taken care of their cats' teeth. So grit your teeth and go after theirs.

Start them young!

It's easier if you get them used to brushing early, regularly stroking the outside of your kitten's gums and mouth to accustom him to having a hand or finger touching his face and mouth.

Then, try actually rubbing his teeth with a clean cloth napkin, or a handkerchief, or cheesecloth dipped in bouillon. Or get a little cotton swab and touch his gums with that. Finally, graduate to (cat) toothpaste and put it on his lips (not in his mouth) to get him used to the taste.

Throughout all this training, keep talking softly and praising him, rewarding him afterwards with some nonfattening goodies. Be careful not to touch his whiskers whenever you go near his mouth.

SHOULD YOU HOLD A CAT
BY THE SCRUFF OF THE NECK?

Their mothers carry kittens by the scruff of the neck, and we are now their surrogate mothers. And you *can* do it to kittens—although the best way to hold a kitten is to support its whole body, resting its paws in the crook of your arm.

But most experts think that the only time you can hold an adult cat by the scruff of the neck is if you're brushing his teeth or doing something directly with his face. Otherwise, the best way to hold a cat is with one hand under his chest and the other under his hindquarters, allowing most of the weight to be in the back.

BRUSHING YOUR CAT'S TEETH (UGGH)

Use a soft child's toothbrush or a special brush manufactured for cats. The upper teeth attract the most plaque so work the hardest there. *Never* use human toothpaste. Cat toothpaste or tooth powder, available from your pet store, veterinarian, or catalog house, is flavored for felines and non-foaming, so he won't gag on it.

If your cat won't cooperate, help is coming! A few products are coming out now that you squirt into your cat's mouth, rub around, and your cat's saliva spreads it around in his mouth. Currently these products are only available at some vet's offices, but hopefully you can soon purchase them in any pet store.

EXAMINING YOUR CAT

Monthly, while you're brushing your cat's teeth—which you should be doing weekly (sure)—breathe in and smell your cat's breath. Hopefully you won't pass out and can do the rest of these tests.

Look at your cat's face and feel the glands on both sides of his neck to make sure each side is equal and there are no abnormal swellings. Pick up the lips and examine his teeth and gums. Check for redness, brown deposits, and broken teeth. Cats are also prone to painful cavities.

If you can't remember to take care of his teeth, when you go to the dentist for your checkup is a good time to have his mouth checked out as well.

How to Clip Your Cat's Claws (She'll Hate You for It!)

Whether she's an indoor or outdoor cat, your cat's claws need to be clipped. Long nails get snagged, causing irritation and infection that can change the normal position of a cat's toes and result in pain and limping. Here are some guidelines:

- Clipping is easier if there are two of you doing it.
- Wrap her in a towel to help control her.
- Work under a bright light.
- Before doing any clipping, pick up each paw and make believe you're clipping without cutting. After a few sessions, your cat will get used to your handling her paws.
- The best way to expose the claws is to press lightly on the top of the paw.
- Except when cutting black claws, you'll see a pink area called the "quick." Cut only up to and not into this.
- Remember that it's better to clip too little than too much.

4 Things You Shouldn't Find When Examining Your Cat

- When you brush your cat's hair against the grain with your fingers, do you find black specks? (Flea excreta.)
- Smell your fingers after running them through its hair; is there a bad or fishy odor? (Bad health.)
- Dark red line along the gum? (Gingivitis or gum inflammation.)
- Do you see the third eyelid? If you do, your cat could be sick or have an eye injury. According to *101 Essential Tips: Cat Care,* if only one eye is showing the third eyelid, it's probably due to the eye itself being injured. If both are showing the third eyelid, then your cat may be sick.

SKUNK SMELL? ODD SOLUTIONS
BESIDES TOMATO JUICE

Massengill douche: This odd solution came from the Internet, where someone in rec.pets.cats suggested giving a skunk-doused cat a bath using traditional baby shampoo, followed by a very untraditional douche solution over the cat's entire body.

The sun: Another suggestion was to put the cat in the sun and the odor will evaporate more quickly. Or try to get your cat in a hot (not scalding) bath with lots of soap.

Peroxide and baking soda: The desired mixture contains 3 percent peroxide, $1/3$ of a cup of baking soda, and 1 teaspoon of liquid soap.

Catsup: If you don't have tomato juice, all is not lost...

---

22. Losing Your Cat— and Finding Her Again

How to Find Your Cat If She's Lost or Stolen, and Keep from Being Scammed Afterwards

Here are some common questions of cat owners about lost or stolen cats.

HOW CAN CATS LEFT SAFELY IN THE BACKYARD DISAPPEAR? If someone doesn't come and take your cat, he can escape when a delivery person opens a gate, he may dig a hole and get out, jump the fence, unhook or break a chain, or unlock a gate.

WHAT HAPPENS TO CATS WHEN THEY'RE STOLEN? It shouldn't happen to a dog—or cat. They may be used for research, animal sacrifice, even food.

DOES TATTOOING CATS HELP? Sometimes. Researchers won't take an animal that has a tattoo or microchip, and will sometimes try to trace him.

WHAT'S THE BEST TIME TO SEARCH FOR A MISSING CAT? Go out daily but especially at dusk or dawn, when he may be out looking for food.

SHOULD YOU OFFER A REWARD AND HOW MUCH? Yes, offer a reward, and larger ones work better. People who pick up your cat may justify keeping it, convincing themselves that if the cat had owners, they didn't really care because he was unleashed or had no collar. A large reward may convince them that you really do want your cat back.

HOW CAN YOU BE SCAMMED FOR MONEY IF YOU DON'T OFFER A REWARD? Someone may call claiming to be an out-of-town trucker who drove through the area, found your cat on the highway, and now needs money to send it back or pay for veterinary bills.

Or a con person may ask for an airline ticket to send your cat back, and then cash in the ticket.

HOW CAN PEOPLE WHO DON'T HAVE YOUR CAT CONVINCE YOU THAT THEY DO? They'll call and say, "Does your missing cat have a black spot on its left ear?" You may say, "No. My cat has a brown spot on its right ear." Later, their *confederate* calls, saying they have a cat with a brown spot on its right ear. You think they have your cat and send them the money they ask for.

HOW CAN YOU TELL IF THE PERSON CALLING YOU REALLY HAS YOUR CAT? First, try asking him something *wrong*, like "Does the cat you found have a black spot on its tail?" when your cat doesn't. Second, always hold back some small identifying characteristic in your ad or poster, so you can see if the person calling you knows it and really does have your cat. Finally, if people claim they need money to pay a vet who treated your cat, call the vet. Even if the vet exists, he or she may not know anything about this situation.

---

5 UNUSUAL IDEAS FOR FINDING A LOST CAT

1. Look all over your house before searching your neighborhood. Cats are often someplace at home and their owner didn't realize it.

2. Take off your shoes and walk back and forth barefoot near the door of your house. Your cat may be able to smell it. (Hopefully, not because the smell of your feet is so strong, but because the cat's sense of smell is so strong.)

3. Sprinkle her (preferably used) kitty litter outside, or put the actual litter box outside.

4. Carry your cat's food with you when you look for your cat. Open up a can, or if it's dry, put it in a tin can or something that will make noise, and rattle and shake the can when walking around looking for her.

5. Leave a piece of used clothing outside, like a shirt recently worn by the cat's favorite person in your household.

HOW SHOULD YOU ARRANGE TO MEET WITH SOMEONE WHO CLAIMS TO HAVE YOUR CAT? Always meet your informant in a public place since you'll be carrying cash.

IS THERE ANY WAY OF INCREASING YOUR CHANCES OF FINDING YOUR CAT? Keep up-to-date photos of your cat. Of course she was adorable as a kitten, but a kitty photo won't help you now if she's missing and ten years old. Make a list, today, of colorings and the

---

HERE'S SHERLOCK BONES

You've heard about him, read stories about him, and seen movies based on his life. Now, if you need him, here's how to find John Keane, Tracer of Lost Pets.

Before you call him—and hopefully you'll never have to—you should know that John will not comb the neighborhood for your cat. He told us that he will do a search through the Internet, or put together a quick poster for you, and mail queries to places where your cat may be, such as neighbors, shelters, and vets.

His phone number is 1-800-942-6637, or contact him through his Web site: http://www.sherlockbones.com

---

location of all markings on your cat. Always make sure he wears a collar with identification on it, and make sure it's secure but not too tight. You should be able to slip two fingers under it but no more.

DO THOSE NATIONWIDE REGISTRIES OF LOST CATS WORK? The problem is that most registries *mail* notices out to shelters, and the notices arrive too late to stop shelters that dispose of pets in forty-eight to seventy-two hours. You can probably get to your cat faster than they can. Also, your cat may have had a major injury and need expensive medical help that the shelter can't afford, so they may dispose of him sooner.

WHOM SHOULD YOU CALL OR CONTACT IF YOU'RE LOOKING FOR YOUR CAT? Slap up *hundreds* of fliers at eye level and put them up within a ten block area of where your cat disappeared. Alert the police, neighbors, shopkeepers, UPS delivery man, construction workers, and limo drivers. Also, talk to people walking with dogs because they'll be the most concerned about pets.

Call local shelters and "pet" places within a hundred mile radius of your home, listed in your phone book under Humane Society, ASPCA, shelters, animal control, veterinarians, etc. Call local schools and see if you can get them to say something on the PA system. Children run around the neighborhood and may spot your cat.

Finally, if your cat disappears, it's important not to be so desperate that you do something foolish. As Sally Fekety, a spokesperson for the Humane Society of the United States, explained to us: "When you lose a pet, your brain isn't on right, and it's easy for people to take advantage of you. You don't hear about some of these crimes because people are hesitant to say afterwards, 'I was an idiot and gave a stranger $100.' Never give anybody any money until you see your cat."

8 Hiding Places for Your Lost Cat— Right in Your Own Home

- In reclining chairs, inside the ledge that supports the footrest when it's out
- In a hole in the boxspring or mattress
- Behind the books in a bookcase
- Behind unopened drawers in a dresser
- In the chimney
- In heating ducts
- Behind the refrigerator
- Wrapped in the bottom of drapes

CHOOSING THE RIGHT CAT COLLARS AND WHAT TO PUT ON THE ID TAG

- Get a collar with a breakaway or escape feature and make sure that it releases quickly in case your cat gets caught on something.
- Don't just put your home telephone number on the tag, but include as many relevant numbers as you can fit on it, along with the number of a registry if you signed up for one.
- Pets generally cannot be traced through their rabies tags, so don't rely on them to help you be reunited with your cat.
- Put the word "Reward" on the tag.

Do Electronic Fences Work?

One cat owner did an experiment with his four cats and put up an electronic fence. The first cat sailed through the fence at full speed.

The second walked to the fence slowly, crawled under the wire, and showed no sign of reacting to the current.

The third made contact with the electrified fence with her nose and ran back to the house. (One success.)

The fourth cat also touched the wire with her nose—and went right through the fence to freedom.

So much for the electrified fence.

That electrified fences don't always work on cats is only one problem. They're also very expensive, as much as $500 to fence a yard.

Worse still, they hurt your cat. If the shock *didn't* hurt, it wouldn't work.

Also, since electric fences are only designed to keep animals in, dangerous—possibly even rabid—animals could get into your yard.

But perhaps the biggest danger is that the electrified fence gives the person who has put it up a false sense of security that their pet is home safe in the yard while the person is away. After all, there are full-page ads for these products all over the place and if the fences didn't work well, would the company continue to sell them and people continue to buy them? (Yes.)

So, people spend $500 plus and go off, confident that their cat is safe in their yard. But if a strong stimulus like a queen in heat passes, your little boy is outta there in a flash.

Save your money—and save your cat. The next time you see the ubiquitous ads, just turn the page.

Tattooing and Microchipping Your Cat

Although in the future all house pets may be tattooed, not enough of them are tattooed or microchipped right now to make it a fool-proof method of finding them.

For example, with microchips, your lost cat will only be reunited with you if the place that finds it has a scanner, and specifically goes looking for a chip, *and* your chip is the same kind read by the scanner. Three big ifs, since many places don't have scanners, don't look for a chip, and all chips can't be read by all scanners.

Tattooing also has its problems, again because most people don't think to look for one. Even if they do look, the tattoo could be hidden by fur, or list only a registry number, so the finder wouldn't know who to call. Even worse, the tattoo could be on the ear of the animal, and a thief could have cut it off. It happens.

Still, doing something to protect your cat is better than doing nothing, so you should have your cat microchipped in the groin area with a registered ID number.

Don't tattoo a kitten, though, because the numbers may get distorted as he gets older. In addition, your cat should wear a tag that indicates that he has been tattooed or microchipped, and how to get in touch with you if it's not obvious from the markings or chip.

Just remember that most lost cats brought to animal shelters don't come home again, mostly because few have identification on them.

Moving with Your Cat—without Losing Her

Edward Lear, author of *The Owl and the Pussycat,* had his second house built to exactly the same specifications as the first so that his beloved tabby cat, Foss, would immediately feel at home.

Chances are you can't do that, and it's also likely that when you move, your outdoor cat will want to go back to the old place. If it's near enough, you'll have to be careful, or the people who move into your old house may end up with a new cat (yours).

A good tip in this area appeared in a column by Ann Landers. A reader's cat kept going back to their old house, so after allowing the cat to get used to the new house a bit, the owner rubbed butter or margarine between the cat's toe pads. The cat licked the butter off, getting accustomed to the scent of his new territory, and never ran away again.

Here are some other things you should know if you and your cat are going to be changing residences:

Moving Day: Try to get someone else to take care of your cat or board him for the day. If you're going to keep him home, put a collar on him and keep it on all day.

Put him in a small room so he won't hide or get out during the continual opening and closing of the outer door. Don't let him out until the movers have left and you're sure all the doors and windows are closed.

The first day in the new home: Don't expose your cat to the whole place at once. Close him in a room with a litter box and other familiar items, such as clothes with your scent on them. Visit him frequently.

Keep his stress down by feeding him on the same schedule, even if you're changing time zones. He doesn't know that it's nine in his new place if his stomach tells him it's noon and that's when he's usually fed.

The first week: Try not to let him outside. If he disappears, look in your old place.

23. Fascinating Facts about Felines

A Cat-alog of 22 of the Most Surprising and Interesting Facts and Figures about Cats

- The average mass-produced cat meal is the nutritional equivalent of eating five mice.
- Canned cat food is calculated to have the same proportion of liquid in it as mice and other cat prey—about 80 percent.
- Cats recognize dog breeds. If they're raised with certain kinds of dogs, they may not be frightened of others of that breed, but may be scared by other breeds of dogs.
- Cats can donate blood to other cats.
- Only the cat, the camel, and the giraffe walk by using the front and hind legs on one side and then the front and hind legs of the other.
- The cat is the only clawed animal that walks on his claws instead of his paw pads.
- Some white cats, especially blue-eyed or odd-eyed cats, suffer from congenital deafness.
- All cats are born with blue eyes.
- There are almost no entirely black cats, although they were once very common. Usually they have some white coloration because totally black cats were considered evil and bad luck and were not kept or bred—or worse.
- Cats have four kinds of hairs which correspond roughly to under, middle, and protective coats, and whiskers.
- A cat's tongue is scratchy because it's lined with papillae—little elevated backwards hooks that help hold prey in place.
- Cats scratch not to sharpen their claws but to shed the sheaths

DO CATS REALLY HAVE 9 LIVES?

One reason cats are reputed to have such longevity is their remarkable ability to survive falls from great heights. Surprisingly, though, they may do better on longer falls than shorter ones, because it takes time for them to position themselves correctly, spreading their bodies out like parachutes so they can land correctly.

In one classic study, cats that fell from the twelfth floor of a building had a 30 percent better chance of surviving than those that fell from the sixth floor.

of the old claws. This process is said to be like sharpening a pencil.

- Cats have trouble climbing down trees because all their claws point in one direction—forward—which is perfect for climbing up. Since cat toes and muscles aren't flexible, a cat can't climb down.
- Although we're more than ten times the size of cats, we have about the same number of bones. Most of their bones are in their tails.
- More American homes have either cats or dogs living in them than children living at home.
- There are about sixty-two million cats in America.
- Almost half of all households with cats own two or more of them.
- There may be as many as twenty-five million homeless cats in the United States.
- A twelve-year-old cat may have spent as many as three years of its life grooming itself.
- A fifteen-year-old cat may have only "lived" five to seven years, because he's spent ten years sleeping.
- A cat has 120,000–130,000 hairs per square inch on its belly.
- 99.99 percent of all calico cats are females.

"Test" Your Cat to See If This Is True

The standard legal disclaimer applies to these tests. We're not responsible for what happens if your cat doesn't like some of them.

- Eat a peppermint patty and then blow in your cat's face lightly and watch what happens.
- Cats have over thirty different ways of saying "meow." How many do you recognize in your cat?
- The pupils of a cat's eyes may enlarge as much as four times as the cat approaches food.
- Breathe into your cat's ears, eyes, nose. It tickles him.
- Rub a coin across a comb quickly enough to produce a noise. Do this in front of your cat, and he may start licking his lips.
- Cats find it threatening to be stared at. If you stare at yours, he may quickly blink or turn his head away from you.
- Your cat is either right-pawed or left-pawed. Can you tell which?
- Try catching your cat's eyes. Then close yours slowly and open them again slowly, all the while looking at him.

The Truth about Cats: Myth or Reality?

1. Cats and dogs can't get along.
   False. If they're raised together, cats and dogs can get along well.

2. All Persians look pretty much the same.
   False. There are more than fifty different colors of Persian cats.

3. Cats naturally kill mice and rats.
   False. No, they naturally *chase* them. They have to learn from their mothers when they're kittens to kill and eat what they've captured. Some turn rodents into toys; others into meals.

4. Cats can see in the dark.
   False. There must be some light. They use their sensitive noses, ears, and whiskers to navigate, but can't see in total darkness.

A FEW WORDS ABOUT WHISKERS

- Cats may also use their whiskers to tell if their prey is dead. A cat with a mouse in his mouth may touch it with his whiskers and see whether it's moving and if it's safe to put the mouse down without it running away.
- Even with closed eyes, cats can sense a mouse from air currents on their whiskers.
- Cats are farsighted, and whiskers may help them navigate when things are close and out of focus.
- Cats whiskers are wider than their body. Cats use them like feelers to see if they'll be able to fit through narrow places.
- Cats have whiskers not only around their cheeks, chin, and eyes, but also in back of their front legs.

---

5. Cats can always see better than people.
   False. During the day, people see better than cats.

6. Cats are fine in hot and cold outdoor weather.
   False. Actually, their fur coats aren't that protective.

7. Cats rub their paws against you because they think you're their mother.
   True. Kittens stimulate the flow of milk by kneading against their mother. They've transferred this caring motion to you, their surrogate mothers.

8. Some cats have extra toes.
   True. Most cats have eighteen toes: five on each of the front paws, and four in the back. But some cats (such as Teddy Roosevelt's) have six and even more toes.

   Certain cats are more likely to have this condition. The Russian blue, for example, and cats from Boston, Massachusetts. It's said that this goes back to Boston's early settlement, when sailors may have chosen extra-toed animals on ships as ratters or pets.

A FEW CAT RECORDS

- The oldest cat lived thirty-six years.
- One breeding pair, allowing for fourteen kittens in three litters a year, could produce 65,536 cats in five years.
- A Burmese cat once gave birth to nineteen kittens in a litter—although four were stillborn.
- The most kittens produced in a lifetime was 420.
- The most mice known to have been killed by a cat was 22,000 in twenty-three years.
- The heaviest cat ever weighed more than forty-five pounds.
- A Siamese fell 1,100 feet from a light airplane and survived.

4 Odd Ways the Weather Affects Your Cat

Leonore Fleischer reported that when George IV was still Prince of Wales, he made a bet with a friend that they would see more cats on the right-hand side of the street they were approaching than they would see on the left.

The prince won the bet because the prince knew that the cats would choose to go over to the sunny side of the street and the sun was on the right-hand side.

Here are a few other odd facts about cats and the weather:

- Cats shed more in the light. Even the glow from a television set can cause more cat hair to fall out.

- Cats groom more in the sunlight. Perhaps depositing saliva helps to reduce the heat.

- Cats in colder climates tend to be larger, the better to hold body heat.

- Cats eat more in cold weather and less when it's hot.

24. Cats versus Dogs, People, Birds, and Mice

Cats Are Better Than Dogs or People Because...

CATS ARE BETTER THAN DOGS BECAUSE...

- Cats make ten times more different vocal sounds than dogs make.
- Cats can watch a moving object better.
- Cats don't have to be walked.
- They can usually outrun dogs their own size or larger.
- Senile cats function better than senile dogs.

> ### CATS VERSUS DOGS
> #### by Dusty Rumsey
>
> Dogs can't perceive television images.
> Cats demand input on which shows to watch.
> Dogs like to sleep at the foot of the bed.
> Cats like to sleep at the head of the bed.
> Dogs mark their territory.
> Cats assume all territory is theirs.

- They have much better peripheral vision and can see things from the side that dogs can't.
- They're more dexterous with their paws.
- It can take months to housebreak a dog—and minutes for a cat.
- They usually live longer.

- Cats cost much less a year to keep—under $500—compared to a dog, which costs more than $1,000.
- They have more sophisticated taste buds.
- They have more secrets.

Cats are better than people because...

- They can jump more than five times their height; we can't even make it once.
- They can hear sounds an octave-and-a-half higher than we can.
- They can fall many more stories and live.
- They're much more concerned with keeping themselves clean.
- They're super sniffers, with a far better sense of smell.
- They have a much better sense of direction.
- They can predict earthquakes and some storms.
- They can run faster than a human sprinter.
- They have nine lives, and we have one.

2 Big Reasons Cats Are Different Than Dogs

First, cats are loners. They hunt alone and don't need help because one cat can handle one mouse. Dogs hunt in packs because they go after prey bigger than they are. Since dogs need each other, they're more social, while cats don't have to be nice to others, including you.

Second, dogs solicit food from their mothers when they're young by licking them. Cats don't. So when dogs grow up they will continue to slobber all over you to show their love, while most cats couldn't care less about kissing you.

Treating Birds and Mice Kindly
Instead of Letting Your Cat Catch Them

Cats may kill as many as half a billion birds and mammals annually—and the alternative may be almost as disturbing to those who have watched their cats seemingly torture a mouse they've caught instead of killing it.

Here are some ways to keep your cat from getting its paws on the prey:

BIRDS

Don't get a birdhouse, and if you have one, put it somewhere your cat can't see it. Don't let the grains of bird food fall from the birdhouse to the ground, where they will attract your cat. Keep grass cut short so your cat can't stalk birds and other prey. Keep a bell on your cat's collar so birds are warned when your cat is coming. (Although many people do this to save the birds, some experts say that bells on cat collars disorient your cat and are therefore not a good idea.)

Stuff your cat. Dr. Peter Neville, one of Britain's most famous animal behaviorists, and the author of *Do Cats Need Shrinks,* calls this the "Alcatraz tactic"—feeding your cat a good meal of favorite foods before letting him go out so he's less tempted by additional prey. The name comes from the fact that Alcatraz used to feed inmates a lot of fattening foods to make it harder for them to be able to swim across San Francisco Bay if they escaped.

Neville says you can also get a cat from a nonhunting mother and keep it indoors and unexposed to rodents and birds until he's about a year old. By that time, cats tend to be uninterested in them and, if they do care, are often unable to capture them.

MICE

A few of the above ideas might also work for mice. But here are some really unusual ideas to save mice that appeared in *Kids Can Save the Animals—101 Easy Things to Do.*

Instead of buying a trap for a mouse or letting your cat sic 'em, get a humane trap, put peanut butter on it, and place it where you've seen mouse droppings. Check back frequently to prevent dehydration should a mouse be caught, and release the mouse outside in a bushy field when you find one.

Then, they suggested you release any mice you find afterwards in the same area so the mouse can be with his friends, and don't let him outside in the winter since mice can freeze outside.

If that's what you want to do, okay, but just remember that if cats weren't so good at killing mice, you never would have a cat for a pet today. Cats became popular as pets because they did such a good job of getting rid of rodents.

Secondly, before you're too humane to mice, remember that two of them in just one-and-a-half years can be responsible for 4 1/2 million more mice, overrunning your house and squeaking up a storm.

25. How Smart Is Your Cat— and Teaching an Old (or New) Cat Tricks

How Smart Is Your Cat, and How to Make Him Smarter

For starters, he's smart enough to have gotten you to support him, and he's probably trained you, too. For example, if he finds you in the kitchen, does he meow to get you to give him a little food? And do you?

WHO'S SMARTER: YOU OR YOUR CAT? If you think of all the times your cat has outsmarted you…. Interestingly, a cat's brain weighs 1 percent of its total weight and ours weighs 2 percent! That doesn't mean we're twice as smart as a cat is, but it is interesting.

ARE SOME CATS SMARTER THAN OTHERS? Of course; some people are smarter than others, too. But whether the cat is a purebred or a mixed breed doesn't seem to matter. In fact, the smartest cat was a mixed stray who knew seventy-five tricks.

Can Cats Remember—and Tell Time?

Yes, cats can recall events—and the memories can last their whole lives. A cat mistreated by a young child early in his life may avoid children for the rest of it.

Generally, though, cats' memories are best for smells. For example, a cat who has a bad experience at a vet may become agitated the minute he comes close enough to the office to smell it.

Still, while cats can remember, they also only remember what's useful for them, like where something they want is, or where they shouldn't go. (Sometimes.)

Amazingly, though, cats frequently don't remember their own kittens. If a mother meets one of her kittens later in life, there is no evidence she remembers him. And the fathers are even worse!

As for time, for cats it's measured in events and happenings, not in numbers. They don't know whether it's 5 o'clock or 5:30. But they often know when it's time for them to be fed, or for their owners to come home, or other pleasurable things.

Can you make a cat smarter? Yes, you *can* teach an old cat new tricks. Handling him, playing with him, and providing him with a variety of different stimuli can make a big difference. Obviously it's better to start younger, but as another cliché goes, it's never too late.

Which are smarter: dogs or cats? Tactful behavioral experts answer the question by saying that "dogs are better at being dogs and cats are better at being cats."

What proof is there that a cat is smart? Lots, but just one example is that most cats learn their names and other words that are meaningful to them, often those related to food or play. Some cats can learn as many as fifty words.

Teach Your Cat to Come When You Call and to Wave Hello

One of the most famous animal trainers in the country, "Captain" Haggerty, author of *How to Get Your Pet into Show Business,* told us how you can easily teach a cat to come to its name—and wave hello.

To come when you call her: Say your cat's name and "come" when you pet her, feed her, or play with her, and she will come to associate pleasant things with her name—like eating and getting petted. Then she'll come when you call her name, or even if you just say "come." *Usually.*

Also, don't use her name if you scold her for doing something wrong, since you don't want her to have any negative associations with it.

To wave hello: While you're training her, whenever you feed her, hold some food out of her reach so she has to stretch her leg to get it. As she does this, tell her to "wave."

Later, she will "wave" when you tell her to, thinking she will be getting food. Put your paw in her hand if you want her to shake hands "hello."

TRAINING YOUR CAT TO JUMP THROUGH A HOOP

This was explained in *Men's Health* by the famous animal trainer for Ringling Bros. Barnum and Bailey Circus, Gunther Gebel-Williams.

Put your cat on a chair next to a chair with food your cat likes on it. Your cat will jump to the food. After she's done that, move the chairs farther and farther apart every few days. Then, introduce a hoop, holding it steady between the two chairs.

It's that simple—he claims! Sure!

---

26. Showbiz and Your Cat

Your Cat Can Win $100,000 on "America's Funniest Home Videos"

All your cat may have to do is be his adorable self while you capture that moment on video and send it to the program. "It has to be a funny or creative or amazing scene," explained Thia Dearwater, a spokesperson for *America's Funniest Home Videos.* "For example, we had a little black cat squeezing under a tiny space in a white door. Another one where a cat jumped four feet to turn on a light switch. Cats are truly amazing," she said in awe.

Her favorite segment was "The Static Cling Cat." "A little guy named Levi crawled into a box with styrofoam peanuts and came out with them clinging all over his fur," she laughed.

Surely your cat could do *that.* Alas, they probably won't want the same routine again, but send in something that's just as cute. Don't spend the money just yet though. Although in the eight years of the show they've given away four million dollars, 1,500 people send videos each week.

Still, a $100,000 winner *was* a cat—and all he did was get bitten on the rear by a bird, shocking him to such a degree that he did a full back flip. So start working on that (not biting your cat, but getting him to do the back flip). Seriously, "Whatever your cat does should happen spontaneously," Thia stressed. "Don't add anything to the video. If we choose it, we will enhance it with sound effects and Bob Saget's voice-overs."

One other important point. "We encourage people to treat pets well and for them to be safe. So, before we show the segment, they must sign a waiver that no one was hurt and it wasn't staged."

Send your video to *America's Funniest Home Videos,* Post Office Box 4333, Hollywood, CA 90078. Include a note with your name, address, phone number, and a brief description of the clip. If you want them to return the video, enclose $3 check or money order made out to *America's Funniest Home Videos.*

How to Place Your Cat on David Letterman's "Stupid Pet Tricks" and Other TV Segments

If your cat did something extraordinary at home last week, he probably won't get on Stupid Pet Tricks. He's got to be able to do the same thing every week, and do it away from home under highly stressful conditions to get on the show. Susan Hall Sheehan, the segment producer, told us that "I've seen more cats *not* do their 'tricks' and ignore and escape their owners than actually perform their tricks in an unfamiliar audition."

Furthermore, the cat that does "nothing" might have a better chance of getting on than the cat that does "something." "Some of our best tricks call for pets to do nothing, like the cat that liked to be vacuumed, or the cat that balanced things on its head. All they had to do was stay still," she said.

"Other reliable cat tricks that have made it onto the *Late Show* are the purely silly things your cat does all the time, like the kitten whose back legs would go into the air when he ran after something, so he'd run for a second or two on his front paws. Or the talkative cat who continued talking even when he ate, thus making it clear for us to hear him saying 'yum yum yum.'"

The problem for you is that even if your cat does the trick at home, he may not do it at a studio, and on command. "Your cat may have a great trick, but when he gets here, he has no clue as to what it is that he's supposed to do. There's so much else going on, that doing his trick may be the farthest thing from his mind. Add to that the fact that your cat can't be bribed—like dogs—when they are in strange surroundings and you can see how difficult it is."

To protect the show from no-dos, generally six animals are brought in for a pet trick segment, while only three or four actually appear on the show. That may cause the owner to lose heart or face, but never any money. The owners of all pets chosen for the segment receive travel expenses, plus $200 or so to cover incidentals for the day, which is spent rehearsing.

If you think your cat has a trick that could cut it, it must also be safe and enjoyable for your cat. That means no spinning your cat on the floor and calling it "break dancing," or cats putting out cigarettes, or cats that are manipulated to look like people or creatures.

Still think your cat can cut it? Susan suggests you "try the strange location test. This is done by taking your cat to someone else's house where he has never been before. Then, turn on the TV for noise and visual distraction and immediately try your trick. Most likely your cat will crawl under the nearest piece of furniture."

If your cat passes the strange location test, call 212-975-5950 and leave a description on Ms. Sheehan's voice mail of what your cat can do. She'll call you back if she's interested. She'll either ask you to attend a live audition or have you send an audition on videotape to: *The Late Show*, 1697 Broadway, NY, NY 10019, attention Stupid Pet Tricks/Susan Sheehan.

They like videotapes in this department, which receives about 150 mail and video applications each week. "Have your cat do its trick a few times in a row without stopping or editing so we can see that the cat is consistent," she said. "And if you really want to impress us with your cat's ability to perform outside of the home, tape it at a public location."

A cat that does something outrageous may get on other shows as well. For example, Jay Leno had a professionally trained cat on his program that could ride a dog's back, swing on a trapeze, roll on a ball, and jump through a hoop. Now, if he could have done it all at one time, he could probably have been on the tabloid shows, too.

How to Make Your Cat a Movie or TV Star

Perhaps you've been watching a commercial in which a cat scratches her fleas and you've been thinking, "Heck, my cat does that at home for free." The difference: That cat doesn't have any fleas. She's probably been trained to scratch herself when she gets an off-camera cue.

Whether your cat could become a celebrity depends on her appearance, abilities, and temperament—yours, as well as hers.

Here are a few other things you should know:

- Don't be a stage mama if you go to an audition. You may be scrutinized as carefully as your cat. Since they often send the owner out of the shoot, they look for people who are quiet, intelligent, poised, and don't seem overanxious.

- Unless they're shooting something for Halloween, it is a probable disqualification for you if your cat is black. Black cats are

---

COULD YOUR CAT DO A COMMERCIAL?

A company called Critters of the Cinema has trained cats in commercials to climb ladders, barrel roll, go down slides, and put basketballs through hoops, according to *Pet Life*, a new pet magazine.

Generally, Critters and such places get their cats from shelters and start training them from scratch. But there is always some room in this business for a well-trained cat because more are needed for one commercial than you realize. If you see a cat do a series of amazing tricks, it's often a series of amazing cats each doing one trick, because teams of look-alike cats are used to create what looks like one cat doing everything.

What's Critters best secret for training cats? They don't feed the cat a big meal before a stunt because then the cat will just nap and have no incentive. They get the cat to do the tricks by rewarding them with food as they go along.

---

generally not chosen because it's too hard to see their features against a light background.

• It's better to live in New York or Hollywood, where most commercials and advertisements are produced, but if you live elsewhere, there may still be work in local advertising and catalogs—which could lead to bigger things.

• Look up "Animal Rental" in the Yellow Pages or *Kemps International Film and Television Yearbook*. Send each agency a description of your cat and what she does, along with a good head shot and another photo of her performing the task.

• Don't tranquilize your cat before an audition or shoot, because that can cause unexpected reactions. If your cat can't respond

---

THE 10 BEST FAMILY CAT MOVIES ON VIDEO

Ever since Felix the Cat bewitched audiences with his animated antics in the twenties, cats—live and otherwise—have fascinated animal fanciers at the movies. Each of the following pictures is available for home video rental, and some are available for purchase.

The Aristocats (animated, 1970, Disney)

The Cat from Outer Space (Sandy Duncan, MacLean Stevenson, 1978, Disney)

Gay Purr-ee (animated, 1962, Warner Bros.)

Harry and Tonto (Art Carney, Ellen Burstyn, 1974, Fox Video)

The Incredible Journey (1963, Disney)

Milo and Otis (1989, Columbia)

Oliver and Company (animated, 1988, Disney)

That Darn Cat (Dean Jones, Dorothy Provine, 1965, Disney)

The Three Lives of Thomasina (Karen Dotrice, Patrick McGoohand, 1963, Disney)

Tom and Jerry: The Movie (animated, 1993, Family Home Entertainment)

---

correctly in a strange environment, with people milling and shouting around her, other animals standing nearby, and lights flashing and focusing at her, find another career for her.

- If you're angling for a cat food commercial, give her some of the product for a few days before the casting so she won't reject it. If she doesn't like it at first, introduce it to her slowly so she's salivating at the audition.

- Forget the "grunge" look. Photogenic cats are generally chosen over a weird look.

- Learn how the business operates. If you want your cat to be a star, or even a spokespet for a product, know the difference between the producer, the casting director, and the agent.

- You don't need a purebred to succeed. Mixed breeds are more often shown with kids, in all-American settings, or in catalogs with less expensive items.

- Don't expect to get rich. Payment is low and there are no residuals for TV work because animals don't have unions. If you go through an agency, remember that they siphon a healthy but well-deserved commission.

- And finally, expect disappointment. You've only a very slim chance of your cat being chosen because the competition is so beastly.

27. Traveling and Holiday Hell

Vacationing with Your Cat

STAYING IN HOTELS AND MOTELS

Tips from Eileen Barish, author of *Vacationing With Your Pet:*

- If your cat sleeps on your bed, take along a used sheet or favorite blanket for her from home.
- Be considerate of housekeeping and place a towel or mat under the food and water bowls.
- Keep a "Do not disturb" sign on your door and clean your room yourself. Be there when they clean your room.
- Right before you leave for your trip, fill the litter box with fresh litter, which will hopefully encourage your cat to "go" before your departure.
- If you have more than one cat and they get along, buy a carrier large enough for both of them so they have the comfort of each other.

TRAVELING IN YOUR CAR

- If your cat has never or rarely been in a car, take him on short trips to get him used to it before a major journey.
- Cats should be secure and not allowed to jump around or hang out of the window. Keep them in a wire-mesh crate so there's ventilation and they can see. It should be large enough for your cat to stand, turn around, and lie down in.
- Take a blanket from home for your cat and put it in the crate.
- Bring your own food and water supplies so there's less chance of stomach upsets. But don't feed your cat before the trip or he may throw up.
- Carry an up-to-date color picture of your cat with you in case he gets lost.
- His carrier should be lined with a towel to absorb urine.

Flying with or Shipping Your Cat

These tips are from the TW Pets Forum on CompuServe.

PREPARING AND USING THE CRATE OR CARRIER:

• Make sure your USDA-approved shipping crate is marked with contact persons at both the departure and arrival sites and, if possible, at any connection point. Your pet should also be wearing an identification tag on an elastic collar.

• Don't lock the door; airline personnel may need to open the crate in case of emergency.

• Make sure the crate has sturdy handles that won't come off during rough baggage handling.

• Line the crate bottom with some type of bedding—shredded paper or towels—to absorb accidents.

• The crate must have two dishes, one for food and one for water, attached to the inside of the crate and easily accessible to airline personnel. For trips longer than twelve hours, attach a plastic bag containing dry food on the top of the carrier, with feeding instructions for airline personnel.

• Freeze a plastic margarine cup filled with water so the water doesn't splash out during loading but melts by the time your cat is thirsty.

DEALING WITH AIRLINES:

• Be sure to arrive at the baggage area to pick up the animal on time, even before the plane lands. Make sure that the airline personnel know that you are there to pick up a cat.

• Make sure you have time at connections to change planes or there may not be time for the crate to switch planes also.

• Don't fly when it's too cold or too hot. Delays on the tarmac can be fatal.

• Book an early morning or late evening flight to avoid temperature extremes.

Traveling with your cat in the cabin:

- Let the person sitting next to you know before takeoff that you have a cat, just in case they have allergies or phobias.
- Don't just take your cat along. Airlines levy an excess baggage charge for pets traveling in crates in the cabin, and you must make a reservation in advance. Airlines are limited as to the number of pets which can travel in each flight.
- Have your cat checked by a vet before the trip and carry any required documentation.
- Keep her nails clipped so they don't get hooked on the carrier.
- Make sure the crate or Sherpa bag is big enough for your cat to be comfortable.

Simple Tip to Keep from Losing Your Cat While on the Road

Staying at different hotels or motels with your cat? Your cat's collar has your home phone number, but you won't be at home if your cat gets lost and someone tries to call you.

Pet travel expert and author Eileen Barish suggests you remove the matches from the hotel and staple one of the matchbook covers to your pet's collar. If your cat disappears, someone will know where you are and can call and reunite the two of you.

How to Keep the Airlines from Killing Your Cat

As many as seventy pets die each year while being transported in commercial airlines—and many deaths aren't even reported. Furthermore, some cats are permanently injured or lost as a result of their trips, and there are no figures on that. Bud Brownhill of Anaheim, California, the chairman of DO-IT, a pet travel advisory organization, gave us some unique ideas on how to keep the airlines from killing or injuring your animal:

- Talk to a supervisor when you get to the airport and tell him you have an extremely valuable pet in terms of dollars—even if it's a mixed breed. "Otherwise, some baggage handlers couldn't care if you were carrying a rock."

- Personalize your cat to the handlers. Put signs on the crate saying, "Hi! I am a Persian kitten. This is my first trip. Please handle my crate carefully."

- When you board a plane, tell the pilot that you have a cat in the hold worth a lot of money—even if it isn't. Also, tell them to make sure to turn on the heat and pressurization in the cargo compartment. "This is done from the cockpit and some-one may have forgotten to give the pilot that information." Cargo compartments can get as hot as 140 degrees, and intense cold can be just as damaging to your cat.

- Put large strips of red or orange fluorescent material all over the crate "so you can spot it halfway across the airport and your cat won't get mixed up with anything else."

- Put arrows or the words "Top" and "Live Animal" on top of the crate so your cat doesn't fly upside down.

- Put your home addresses and phone numbers, plus those of where you're going, inside and outside the crate, because many people won't reach into a kennel for fear of being scratched or bitten.

- Watch the ticket clerk attach the destination tags at the airport. "Make sure it says 'Detroit' if you're going there."

How to Save Your Cat
If Your Plane Crashes

Officially, in a plane crash, you're supposed to exit immediately when the plane lands and leave all your belongings (including your cat in the crate) behind. Although the following may violate FAA rules, if you want to save your cat, as you realize you're going down, with your seat belt still on, try to immediately pull the cat's crate out from under the seat.

Once you land (crash?), you may only have a few seconds to get yourself out, which will not give you enough time to pull out a crate. It may also be dark and smoky and you won't be able to see.

Furthermore, if you're in the middle or aisle seat and bending down and pulling on a crate, those next to you aren't going to hang around politely waiting. They're going to trample you trying to get out themselves.

Of course we're not recommending this, and we might add that there's only the remotest chance that you will ever have to do this. But perhaps it will keep you calmer if you're traveling with your cat in the cabin and there's an emergency to know that both of you may be able to make it out safely.

- Make certain your pet is loaded last, especially during extreme weather conditions. This may also ensure that he is taken off the plane first.
- Make sure the airline is not carrying dry ice, which can be deadly if your cat is crated near it.
- Avoid flying at the busiest times, so your cat can get more personal attention.
- Ask the airline if you can watch your cat being loaded and unloaded at the cargo hold.

Getting Your Cat in a Crate

The best way to get your cat into a crate is to stand the carrier on its end, with the door open at the top, and lower your cat—facing away from you—into it. Consider wearing gloves.

You should try to get her used to the crate before your first flight. Start by putting food she likes inside, along with her favorite blanket or whatever. Don't put the top on the crate the first time. Then, when she's comfortable, put the top on but not the door. Then put the door on but don't close it.

Incidentally, sedating your cat for the trip is a lazy way to get her to stay in there without protesting. Try the techniques above and avoid sedation unless your vet suggests it.

Get your cat used to hearing airplane noises by taking her for a drive on a busy highway. Otherwise, it's a horror story for an overprotected animal in a cold, unpressurized, noisy crate in an airplane for the first time.

Finally, don't keep your cat in the crate longer than necessary. While waiting around at the airport, you should have something like a Sherpa bag (invented by a pet-owning airline hostess), which has netting around it so your cat can see out.

Scared on the Fourth of July and Fear of Thunderstorms

July Fourth is no picnic for most cat owners, since it causes more animals to stray and panic than any other time of the year. And even plain thunderstorms can turn your generally peaceful quiet pet into a Tasmanian devil.

Calming your cat during the holiday or a bad storm could save her life. Cats, upon hearing the sounds of thunder, or the snap, crackle, or pop of fireworks—especially for the first time—have jumped out of windows, leaped through screen or glass doors, or simply run away to hide, never to be seen again.

What should you do?

- Don't wait until you hear the noise. Remember that cats can hear sounds and feel vibrations that we can't, so prepare early. By the time you realize there are fireworks or a thunderstorm, your cat may have already bolted.

- Try not to leave your cat alone on scary holidays, but stay with her and calm her. See if you can distract her by pulling out some toy she likes and playing with her during the fireworks or thunder.

- Play music. Try soft music, but you might have more luck playing music with a loud percussive beat, like the "1812 Overture," so the fireworks or thunder won't sound as bad, since it won't suddenly burst out from a quiet background.

- Close the windows and pull the blinds so the thunder won't be heard and the lightning won't be seen.

- Speak to your vet about a little Valium. Alternatively, keep her confined in a crate.

- Unless your cat's a real diehard outdoor cat, bring her inside so the noise doesn't cause her to react unnaturally—like disappearing—and she isn't harmed by a prankster or cat hater who throws fireworks at her.

Other dangers to watch out for: Burns, eye damage, hearing loss, and even deafness from fireworks can occur if your cat gets too close to an explosion. Fireworks can also explode if a cat chews on them.

If you're the one setting them off, dispose of fireworks properly. Don't set them off too near windows. You don't want your cat choking on leftover fragments or swallowing them and developing digestive problems and serious injuries.

Why Christmas May Not Be So Merry for Your Cat

Deck the halls with boughs of holly—but watch out for that and other plants and bushes if you have a cat. And, 'tis the season to be jolly—but not always for your cat, who risks a number of holiday hazards. For example:

- Those Yule logs on the fire may look warm, but a flying ember could make it dangerously hot for your cat if her coat is singed or burned.
- She can also burn her paws if she gets too close to the fire.
- The tree may represent gifts for your family, but it could mean trouble for your cat if she climbs on it and knocks it over, or gets pine needles in her paws.
- The water under the Christmas tree may have additives that are poisonous.
- The tinsel could saw her insides, and pine needles could puncture them.
- She might try to swat the small ornaments on the tree, or chew the small hooks that hang the ornaments, or bite the light cords.
- If you celebrate Chanukah, potato pancakes mean hot oil, and dreidels can be swallowed.
- Perhaps your guests or their children might think it's cute to give your cat lots of alcohol, like eggnog, and she may become comatose.
- Your cat may also find plenty of bad things to eat on her own without anyone's help, like skin and bones, or the twine used to truss the turkey. Cats especially like flavored string.
- Even if guests and children don't feed, upset, or try to play with your cat when she doesn't want to, they can disturb her normal routine. Most cats don't like all those strangers around. Outsiders can mean doors opening and closing, and your cat can slip out.

- Not all guests tolerate cats, so yours may have added stress by being banished someplace due to an allergic mother-in-law or an anti-cat college chum.
- You'll also have less time to care for your cat and play with her during the busy holiday season, which can add to her stress.

Here are a few additional things to watch out for so that Christmas doesn't turn out to be "bah humbug" for your cat and you: • When you leave a room with a Christmas tree, unplug the lights and be sure your cat is out of there. • Keep the screen on in front of the fireplace. • Watch what goodies you give her. • Be extra watchful of her environment, especially if you have candles and decorations. • Place dangerous things high. • Use tiny pieces of ribbon instead of hooks to hang ornaments. • Use protective coverings and aversive products on cords to lights. • Anchor the tree to the wall or the ceiling so the cat can't topple it. • Get an artificial tree.

Just remember: Safe Christmases are merry Christmases for your cat.

IT CAN BE HELL-OWEEN FOR YOUR CAT

Happy Halloween it often *isn't* for cats. Here are a few ways to make it safer:

- Keep cats inside the house. Even if they usually stay outside, be sure to bring them in for the entire night—especially if they're black.
- Keep cats in a room far away from the constant ringing of the doorbell.
- Don't give cats any candy, and tell your children to do the same.
- Don't advertise before Halloween to give away a cat—especially a black one.
- Don't put costumes on cats, especially ones with rubber bands.

28. Taking Photos of Your Cat— and Getting Them Published

Taking Photos of Your Cat Is a Snap

Distinguished photojournalist Jill Freedman, who has photographed animals as well as a variety of other subjects, says: "Don't worry about sophisticated equipment, special flash attachments, or elaborate setups. Even if it's a point-and-shoot disposable, take photos of your cat at play, at rest—and doing what he does best, which is just being a cat."

Here are a few of her suggestions:

- Get the cat used to you following him around with a camera. The more you pretend you're taking pictures, the more he'll ignore you when you're into serious photo taking.
- Try shooting at your cat's level. Get down on the floor or put your cat up on a chair or table.

HOW TO PHOTOGRAPH A BLACK CAT

- Don't use a white background, which will increase the blackness and lack of detail in your cat.
- Don't use a black background because it will make the entire scene too dark. A neutral background is best.
- Don't shoot the cat against a wall. If you're using a flash and the black cat is close to the wall, the black shadow behind him will merge into his body.
- Make sure your cat's head doesn't create a shadow.
- One photographer reported good results putting his cat on a yellow sheet.
- Make sure there's lots of light on his face.
- Use good film.

How to Avoid "Red Eye" When Taking Your Cat's Photos

Have photos of your cat been ruined because of the shiny colors that appeared in his eyes? Photographer and owner of two cats, Jill Freedman, says to avoid red eye, "You should hold the flash off the camera, like hold it in your left hand with the camera in your right and put the flash slightly above the camera so it's off center and a little higher than the camera lens. Then you're not shooting directly into the eyes of your subject."

Another way to solve that problem is to buy a newer camera. "Many cameras now, including the point and shoot, have the kind of flash that goes boop boop boop a couple of times so the lens closes down and you don't get the red eye," she says.

- Stay close. Your cat should take up at least half of the photo.
- Keep the area and the background uncluttered. You don't want to distract from your real subject.
- For extra light, "bounce" flashes off the ceiling. Outdoors, keep the sun behind you or to the side.
- Catch your cat in action. Throw him his favorite toy. Don't be afraid to snap the shutter when he's in midleap. One of your experimental in-motion shots is going to be a classic!
- Take lots of breaks, give plenty of treats, shower your cat frequently with praise.
- It's easy to take a picture of a beautiful cat. It's more difficult to capture a cat's personality, and that's what your aim should be.
- Since cats don't follow orders or humor you in the way dogs do, it's up to you to find a way to catch your cat unaware he's performing for you.

But the most important rule Jill gives is "break all the rules! That's how you're most likely to have a memorable picture."

Jill's most recent book, "Jill's Dogs," can be seen and ordered on the Internet at http://www.jillfreedman.com

Magazines and Newspapers That May Print Photos of Your Cat

1. *Animals* charges an entry fee of $10 per photo for their annual contest, which could win you a grand trip to an exotic place. For details where, or an entry form, call 617-541-5107

2. *Cat Fancy* prints 4-6 color photos per issue in their Gallery. On the back of the photo, include your cat's name, your name, city, and state. Cat Fancy Gallery, P.O. Box 6050, Mission Viejo, California 92690.

3. *Cats* magazine has a Paw Prints section which prints several color photos (plus one "Picture of the Month") each issue. Send photo and a brief story of your cat, along with your name and address, to *Cats,* Editorial Department, P.O. Box 1790, Peoria, Illinois 61656.

4. *Cats USA:* Prizes include publication and $150, $100, or $75 for the top three winners. Contest is announced yearly in *Cats USA* and entry forms are in this publication, which is available at larger newsstands.

5. *National Enquirer* Readers Photo Special is often a pet. Prize is $250. Rules are in the newspaper and photos should be sent to National Enquirer Photos, Lantana, Florida 33464.

6. *Workman* Publishing uses more than 100 winning photos in their annual Cat Calendar. Request entry forms from Workman Publishing, P.O. Box 3927, New York, New York 10163.

   NOTE: Most places don't return or acknowledge photos.

HOW TO PHOTOGRAPH A CAT

by Jack Fleming

Put the cat on a pillow.

Set up your camera and focus it on the pillow.

Put the cat back on the pillow.

Get a bowl of food and put it next to the pillow.

Put the cat back on the pillow.

Grab the food bowl and follow the cat. As you run, hold the bowl in your cat's face, tempting her to eat.

See if the neighbors will come over and pick up the sofa while you snap a picture of the cat underneath.

Cross the names of your neighbors off the list for your next party.

Put cat back on the pillow.

Place a catnip-stuffed mouse in front of your cat and wait for your cat to go crazy.

Go back to the pet store and demand a refund.

Decide on a family portrait with the cat instead.

To stop the argument over which child gets to pose with the cat, agree to take pictures of each child holding the cat on his or her lap.

Tell each child that it doesn't matter who holds the cat first because you'll shuffle the pictures after they're developed and look at them in a different order than the order they were taken.

Get more cats, one for each child, and go back to step one.

29. If Your Cat Dies— and How to Prepare Now

Do Cats Go to Heaven When They Die?

Do cats go off to die? Probably not. They want to be alone when they're sick, and go off to find a quiet place. Since they're sick, they may die alone. What happens to them after they die, though, is a question many people have wondered about for centuries. We spoke with five theologians from different traditions.

> *We think of heaven as like looking at a puzzle with some of the pieces missing. We can't solve that puzzle because we can't know what happens until we die and by then we can't call home. Nobody knows for sure if animals are in heaven because nobody knows for sure if animals have souls. They definitely don't have souls exactly like our souls because they can't decide between good and bad.*
>
> *Even though their souls are different, is God's love for animals big enough to bring them to heaven? We believe God loves animals enough to do this wonderful thing for them. So when you die, you may see your cat and dog again—and also your goldfish who you flushed down the toilet—so be careful!*
>
> —Monsignor Thomas Hartman, Director of Radio and Television for the Diocesan Television Center in Uniondale, New York, and coauthor of *Where Does God Live?*
>
> *Most of Judaism focuses on how we act in this world, and there's not too much speculation on what goes on in the next world. We don't know exactly who goes to heaven or why, so maybe cats do go to heaven.*
>
> *Within Judaism, one must be kind to animals, because we will then develop ourselves as kinder and gentler and more*

compassionate human beings, and ultimately treat other human beings with more gentleness and kindness. And we hope that on the basis of treating people kindly, we will go to heaven, or to the world to come, or wherever we go when we die.

—Rabbi Neil Cooper, Beth Hillel-Beth El, Wynnewood, Pennsylvania.

Animals don't have souls so far as we know; I therefore have no mandate for saying whether they will or will not go to heaven. But I have to trust God's kindness that there's something I don't know that makes provisions for that.

The love animals give to humans somehow cannot be lost into nothingness. The fact that He created such a beautiful thing is very obviously part of His pattern and plan for our joy and the joy of humanity.

—Father John Andrew, former chaplain to the archbishop of Canterbury.

Christians generally believe that people go to heaven through their belief in Jesus Christ, and since cats don't believe in Him, they would not. But many Christians like myself do not exclude others from life after death, and we believe there are many different paths to God.

I'm a Methodist minister, and our founder, John Wesley, rode his horse everywhere, preaching. He firmly believed his horse went to heaven, because he loved his horse, who served him faithfully. So, from his point of view, it is possible that he would have made that extension to other pets.

—Reverend Julie Parker, Protestant chaplain at Hofstra University in Hempstead, New York.

Prophet Mohammed, a great cat lover who sometimes preached with a cat in his arms, was said to have cut off the sleeve of his robe rather than disturb his pet cat who was sleeping there.

We are taught that heaven is for human beings, and that when animals die, whether they are cats or dogs, they turn back into dust the way they were before, and that is the end of the animals.

But the way a person treats animals may determine whether that person goes to heaven or hell. Prophet Mohammed said that a sinner who shared water with a thirsty dog, bringing it up from a well in her shoe, went to heaven when she died because of her compassionate act.

But a person who tied their cat up in their house, preventing him from getting food and water so the cat died, went to hell because they prevented the animal from finding its own way to survive.

—Al-Haaj Ghazi Khankan, Director of Interfaith and Communications at the Islamic Center of Long Island, Westbury, New York.

We also asked a theology scholar, Scott S. Smith, author of *Pet Souls: Evidence That Animals Survive Death,* to summarize some of the other religious positions:

Buddhism doesn't say that animals go to heaven, because they don't believe anything survives death except Karma. They're vague about what happens when you achieve Nirvana.

The Hindus are of two minds on the subject but in neither one do you have someone going to heaven. In one form, there is no reality. We don't last, nothing is permanent, and there are no individual souls. So pets do not go to heaven because there's no such thing as pets or human beings.

In another branch, they believe in souls, but they don't go to heaven either. They just get reincarnated in different forms, so your cat may end up as your dog.

Shinto: They believe everything has a soul: rocks, water, and yes, cats and dogs. They will all go to heaven.

In conclusion, he said, "Here there are more animals than people in this world and most religions don't even have anything to say about it. Isn't that incredible?"

The Last Will and Testament of an Extremely Distinguished Cat

Barbara Meyers, certified grief therapist and human-animal bond consultant of the Holistical Animal Consulting Center of Staten Island, New York, wrote these cat's words, which will give comfort to those who have recently lost a cat.

I have little in the way of material things to leave, only my love and magic which I leave to all who have loved me. To my Friend, I know will mourn the most ... to my companions ... I ask them to remember me always but not to grieve for me too long.... Let them remember that no cat was ever happier but I have grown ill and pained. It is time to say "Good-Bye." I accept this part of the journey as a natural part of life.

What will come to me after death? I would like to think that I will be joined by companions I've known in life. I will romp in mice-filled fields and every hour will be mealtime. I will spend long evenings in front of fireplaces with logs forever burning and curl up with memories of the love of my special person.

One last request I make. I ask my friend, for the love of me, to have another. No cat can be as distinguished and handsome as I was, but my friend must not ask the impossible.

To that new cat, I've left my handmade Afghan throw and "stairway to the stars" climbing post. I leave him my place on the window perch which I loved so much, and wish him a long, sunny afternoon of snoozing and bird watching.

A few last words, Dear Heart. I have loved you completely and no matter how deep I sleep I shall hear you. Remember that Angels are not allowed to show their wings on earth, there's no rule against whiskers!

—Shortened version of "Last Will and Testament of an Extremely Distinguished Cat," © 1986, 1996 Barbara Meyers, who offers telephone consultations to those who have lost their cats.

How to Have Your Cat Cared for After You Die

Supposedly, more than one million pets in America have been named as beneficiaries in their owners' wills. Too bad the pets will never see the money. Here are a few things that will work and that owners should know now if they want to be sure their cat will be cared for after they die:

1. No one reading this book would ever consider having his cat put to sleep when he dies, but you might be interested to know that such requests are not carried out by the court anyway.

2. Another solution that may not work is advertising to give your cat away after you die. Sally Fekety of the Humane Society told us that "It's getting to be more common where people answer these classified advertisements posing as buyers, sometimes even coming with a child along, and promising to give the pet a good loving home. Then they sell it for research or worse. It's easier for them than running the risk of stealing an animal and being seen."

3. The best solution is to find a friend or relative *now* who will take your cat after you die—and to discuss it with them *now* rather than surprising them in your will. They may not want your cat or be able to take him. They may be more positive if you leave them some money for food, toys, and veterinary expenses for the rest of your cat's probable life.

4. Add a codicil to your will so the caretaker can take your pet right away, before a formal reading of the will. Also, make sure the caretaker knows your cat's routine, favorite games, food, litter-box type, and veterinary information.

5. You can also leave money to your veterinarian and have him arrange for your cat to be cared for. Discuss this with him or her in advance. You may wish to leave them any remaining money when your cat dies, or have it go to somebody else. Have your lawyer draw up a contract.

6. Never leave money directly to your cats. You can bet that some relative, no matter how remote, is going to sue, and the money may end up with an alternate beneficiary or that cousin you always despised.

7. Most states don't allow trusts for animals. But would you want one? Cats can't go to court to snitch on a trustee who spends his catnip money at the blackjack tables.

8. There are a few places that will take care of your pet if you leave them a large sum of money, say $25,000 or so. You might ask your vet or local humane society if they know of such places.

9. Instead of leaving your money to your cat, if you decide to leave it to an organization that helps other cats, or all animals, if enough money is involved, they may help find your cat a happy home after you die.

Two Unusual "Endings" for a Cat

1. You can have your cat mummified by a company in Salt Lake City for $4,500. They use an updated version of the ancient Egyptian method so your cat will last forever. Summum Mummification, (801) 355-0137.

2. In *The Cat's Pajamas*, Fleischer said that a Buddhist foundation operates a cemetery in Tokyo that cremates your cat or dog when it dies. Then, for a few dollars a year, they keep his ashes until you die, when you and your cat can be interred forever together in the memorial park.

Should You Leave a Cat in a No-Kill Shelter?

No-kill shelters, which don't euthanize their pets, are a wonderful idea in the abstract. But, unfortunately, not enough people in this world have the wonderful idea of adopting second-hand cats, especially older ones. It may take a long time to place your cat in a home from these shelters—if they're taken out at all—so yours could languish in a crate for the rest of its life. Would you really want that for him?

If you're going to leave your cat to a no-kill shelter facility:

- Check carefully exactly what they do about getting unwanted animals out of their premises. Some of them keep pets longer than a regular shelter, but will still ultimately unburden themselves of some animals in unpleasant ways.

- Some only take in strays, so if the cat you're bringing in is or was a stray, make sure they know this.

- These shelters are usually very full for months and years in advance, so try to make arrangements as soon as you feel you may need it.

- Go to see the place. Some of them are quite dirty, and you might not want your cat to stay there even if there were no good alternatives.

30. Legal, Landlord, and Insurance Questions

Questions Most Often Asked Lawyers about Cats

To find out the answers, we spoke to Jeffrey D. Delott, Esq., a New York attorney, who is one of the most famous animal lawyers in the country.

CAN I LEAVE MONEY TO MY CAT? "In more and more states you can. But in most states, you can still only leave money to someone to take care of your cats."

MY CAT WAS ACCIDENTALLY KILLED AND IT WAS ENTIRELY ANOTHER PERSON'S FAULT. WHAT KIND OF DAMAGES CAN I GET IF I SUE? "You can get the market value back, and more and more states are also recognizing the companionship value of your cat, the emotional distress damages that your cat's death may have caused you, and veterinary costs."

CAN SOMEONE SUE ME FOR THE PAIN AND SUFFERING THEY CLAIM MY CAT CAUSED THEM? "Whether it's your car or your cat, they can sue you. If your cat scratched and injured somebody and they became deathly ill with cat scratch fever, they could sue you for millions, the same as if they slipped and fell outside your house.

"They may be able to prove that they needed medical treatments, medication, physical therapy, counseling (to get rid of their fear of cats), and that they sustained a loss of earnings because they couldn't work because their hand was damaged."

MY CAT COST ME A FORTUNE IN MEDICAL EXPENSES THIS YEAR. CAN I DEDUCT HER AS A DEPENDENT? "The IRS doesn't think of your cat as a dependent, or you as 'head of the household' with a lot of cats, even if you do think of yourself in this manner."

My cat became ill at a kennel because of their neglect. Can I sue them? "Yes, they must return the cat in the same condition in which it was delivered. If your cat was injured or killed there, you might have a suit against them."

Since this is a free country, can I have as many cats as I want? "Usually you can in rural areas, but many cities restrict residents to two or three animals per household. In cities, many apartments, condos, and coops also have animal restrictions. Even if you are permitted cats, if they are a nuisance, you may not be able to keep them."

When my cat dies, can I bury her in my backyard? "Although people do, many towns have ordinances against it. It's best to have your vet handle the burial."

I have a cat although it's against my lease. Can I be evicted? "Yes, but if the clause has not been enforced for a long time, the landlord may have lost his or her right to object unless you secreted the cat. But if your landlord knows about the cat for a while, he can't use that as an excuse to make you decide between your apartment or your pet."

What is a lemon pet law? "This is similar to a car lemon law, allowing you to get your money back or get another cat if yours becomes sick or dies after purchasing it. Laws vary in those states that have pet lemon laws so find out what you are entitled to," says Delott.

Is Getting Cat Insurance the Best Policy for You?

The best thing about having pet insurance is not just that catastrophic illnesses are covered, but that you're more likely to have your pet treated for less expensive problems if you're not concerned about what it costs. The largest pet insurance company right now is VPI, and here's the bad news:

- Although they cover 6,000 conditions, they won't reimburse you for pre-existing ailments of your cat.
- Figuring out which coverage you want is confusing since they offer several different plans. The average person pays $165 a year in premiums per pet.
- The company is having financial problems, and many other pet insurance places have gone under in the past.

The good news:

- With their policies, you can go to your own vet.
- They have just come out with a well-care plan (for $99) that will cover discounts on routine prevention procedures—including spaying and teeth cleaning. This should be quite popular,

---

WARNING! YOUR CAT COULD MAKE YOU THE VICTIM OF A CRIME

We sometimes let our guard down in situations involving pets, thinking that anyone approaching us about something so terrific as pets has to be pretty wonderful himself. Criminals know and take advantage of this. For example:

- Two women in California were raped when they let men into their houses to see animals they had advertised to sell.
- People have been robbed when bringing cash to pay rewards to those who claimed they found their lost pet—and didn't.

---

thereby helping them with their financial difficulties. If interested in the insurance, call 1-800-USA-PETS.

Alternative: Put aside money in a special account each week for medical expenses for your cat if you should ever need it.

Persuading Your Landlord to Let You Have a Cat

- If permissible, offer to give them a small additional refundable security deposit which they can keep if your cat does any damage. Your landlord may be able to resist cats, but what landlord can resist extra money?
- Promise to keep your cat's nails clipped, and keep to your promise.
- If your cat is declawed, point this out. This is a big point with many landlords, who will relent if they think the cat can't scratch their property.

31. New Age Cats

Are Cats Psychic?

Some swear that cat clairvoyance is a fact; others say it's all just a tall tale (tail?). But there are many hard-to-explain stories of cats knowing when their owners would return, traveling distances too great not to have some help finding their way, and of cats seeming to know about impending disasters, and sensing dangers to themselves and their owners.

Disbelievers stress that these reports are anecdotal, self-deceptive, or easily explained away. Nonetheless, many highly respected researchers are believers. For example, Dr. Michael Fox writes: "Many animals, possibly your pet included, possess mental (or psychic) abilities far more sensitive and better developed than ours ... [and are] far more aware of ... another dimension of reality that is relatively close to us...."

Another prestigious believer is Dr. Rupert Sheldrake of Cambridge University, who has conducted a study into the invisible bonds between people and animals. He says he has collected two thousand reports of individual experiences of this psychic connection between pets and their owners. He believes these psychic bonds occur when there is a close emotional bond between the owner and their pet.

Dr. J. B. Rhine, formerly at the Institute of Parapsychology, in North Carolina, did a series of experiments on the extrasensory powers of cats, as did Dr. Karlis Osis of the American Society for Psychical Research. Both reported findings of telepathic and clairvoyant powers in cats, claiming that they were able to successfully transfer what was on their minds to their cats.

The best known cases of this psychic bond are "psi trailing," where a cat travels hundreds of miles to be reunited with his owners. Skeptics say the returned cat is a stray that looks like their cat.

Other skeptics say it's really *scent* trailing, and it's possible that cats have sensory abilities that we're not even aware of yet.

For example, for years people talked about "psychic Saint Bernards," dogs who were able to find people buried under snow in an avalanche. Later, it was learned that dogs had "heat detectors" in their noses, and were responding to the heat of the buried person, not their aura.

And cats do have extraordinary sensory abilities. They can hear and smell better than we can, they are aware of small vibrations and changes in static electricity, sensitive to ultrasonic sound, and their whiskers are sensitive to minute movements in the air. Furthermore, they have four legs, not two, touching the ground.

But what about the cat owners who say their cats know when they are coming home? Is this psychic, or are there visual landmarks, smells, and other factors that help guide the cat responsible. For example, the position of the sun, the vibration of the traffic, or the cat's familiarity with the sound of the family car down the block or in the driveway may all provide clues.

Perhaps, as we come to learn more about cats and our environment, cats' "psychic" feats will be explained away in "logical" terms.

Or perhaps not.

How to Find a Cat Psychic

It's hard to know who the top psychics in a particular area are, but there is a book out now called *The 100 Top Psychics in America: Their Stories, Specialties, and How to Contact Them,* which includes a section on animal psychics. This book tells the background and the most interesting stories of several top animal psychics. Photos of each of them are included, along with information on how to reach them, by mail, phone, fax, or E-mail.

Other than that, you're pretty much on your own if you're searching for a psychic with whom to discuss your cat. Here are a few things you should know about this area.

- Psychics have specialties, and because someone has helped your friend with a business question doesn't mean the person will be able to help you with a missing pet, or tell you why your cat hates your Uncle Max.

- A 900 number is the worst place to go to talk to a psychic. Most phone psychics are phone-y psychics—often people reading from prepared scripts who are more anxious to keep you on the phone than to help you with your problem.

- Yellow Pages are also a bad place to find psychics, since anyone can place an ad, and backgrounds aren't checked.

- If you go to a psychic, watch out for those who use vague words and phrases like "maybe" or "it's possible that." Similarly, be wary of people telling you something that has a 50 percent chance of being accurate.

- Beware of broad behavioral statements. Most animal psychics know something about pets, and they may be telling you something based on common knowledge or common sense, rather than on a sixth sense that they claim they have.

One woman spent a lot of money on a cat psychic who told her that her cat was missing the litter box because he was upset over a family problem. Well, you could have learned something like that from this book for free.

7 Natural Products to Use with Caution

- **Mineral oil** shouldn't be given with a spoon or it may go down your cat's trachea and lead to pneumonia.
- **Baking soda:** Brushing your cat's teeth with baking soda or salt doesn't effectively remove plaque. Besides, baking soda contains sodium, which can be harmful to older cats with heart disease.
- **Boric acid:** some use it to get rid of tear stains (also fleas!) but cats lick each other and it can cause problems.
- **Castor or cod liver oil** can produce severe intestinal cramps.
- **Vitamin D** overdose can cause an accumulation of calcium, and possibly cause kidney stones.
- **Brewer's yeast** needs a long period of time to be digested and does little more for your cat than cause gas, according to an article in *Natural Pet* magazine (and they ought to know). It also causes skin allergies in many cats. And, finally, if you're giving it to your cat for fleas, your cat may be scratching as you read this. In other words, it doesn't work.

---

2 Good Natural Products

Natural grass: For some cats, the sharp microscopic barbs on blades of grass create internal problems and too-frequent vomiting. Barley Cat, a powdered health supplement made from fresh barley grass grown without pesticides, shaken on food may be a good alternative. Available at health food or pet stores, or call 1-800-222-3374. 3 oz. = $18.99

A natural remedy for hot spots or lick granuloma comes from Drs. Robert and Susan Goldstein, who say you should take a plantain plant, chop the leaves finely in a food processor, and put them right on the sore spot. You may have to clip the hair from your cat to make contact on that spot, if your cat hasn't bitten it all off for you.

32. Free Info and Web Sites on Cats

10 Free Sources of Information on Cats

BEHAVIORAL AND HEALTH QUESTIONS

1. **San Francisco Behavior Help Line** will help answer questions about behavioral problems. Call 415-554-3075. They may take two days to return your call, collect.

2. **Tree House Animal Foundation Pet Care Hotline:** 773-784-5488 9 A.M.-5 P.M. central time

3. **Free Pet Newsletter:** Doctors Foster and Smith *Pet Pause,* free with their catalog, 1-800-562-7169.

4. **Free E-mail newsletter:** *CATsumer Report.* To subscribe send an E-mail message to majordomo@listserve.cftnet.com and write "SUBSCRIBE CATSUMERREPORT" and your E-mail address.

5. **Free veterinary consultation:** A cat question will be answered free by a veterinarian if you don't mind being on hold for about two years. Just call (along with the other 10,000 people) during a limited time each week at 715-369-2022. Tuesdays and Thursdays 9-12, central time.

6. **Free book catalog:** *The Direct Book Service* contains many cat books (and tapes) you didn't know existed and can't wait to read. Call 1-800-776-2665 for twenty-four-hour delivery.

FREE PHONE COUNSELING SERVICES FOR PEOPLE WHOSE CATS HAVE DIED

7. Tufts Pet-Loss support hotline: (508) 839-7966
8. Chicago Veterinary Medical Association: (630) 603-3994
9. University of California at Davis: (916) 752-4200
10. University of Florida School of Veterinary Medicine: (352) 392-4700 x 4080

Our Favorite Way-Out Cat Books

277 Secrets Your Dog Wants You to Know: A Doggie Bag of Unusual and Useful Information by Paulette Cooper and Paul Noble. Many cat owners also own dogs, so if you liked this quirky book, and you own a dog—or you have a friend who is a dog nut— our dog book is the book to get. $8.95.

Why Cats Paint by Heather Busch and Burton Silver. Help the inner artist in your cat to claw its way out. $14.95.

Menopaws: The Silent Meow by Martha Sacks. There aren't many words, but who needs words when the illustrations (by Jack Davis) are this good? $9.95.

The Whole Kitty Catalog by John Avalon Reed. Filled not only with wonderful things you can buy your cat, and wonderful books you can buy for yourself, but interesting cat facts. By the way, his *Whole Dog Catalog* is also great. $18.95.

How to Live with a Jewish Cat by Sig and Par Heavilin. Includes "Ten Commandments a Cat Will Ignore," and "Psychotherapy for the Meshugge Cat." $10.95. *How to Live with a Jewish Cat #2* is also available. $11.95.

Cats on the Web

More than 500 cats have their own sites on the Internet—and some get as many as 10,000 hits each day. Admittedly, most sites are not maintained by cats, but rather by the people who care for them and love them and know them.

These and thousands of other Web sites answer the needs of cat owners and cat fanciers around the clock. The Internet is full of questions for and answers from veterinarians, poems and prose in praise of pussycats, and fables and philosophies for and about felines. Thanks to computer technology, Webmasters can present a wide range of photographs, drawings, and cartoons that will amuse, entertain, and stimulate any cat lover.

Here's just a sampling of the sites we've explored for you. (Please remember that sites have a tendency to come and go.) In no particular order, these are some of our favorites:

- **The Feline: from Goddess to Pet:** An illustrated history of the cat. http://www.indiana.edu/~eric_rec/fl/pcto/feline.html

---

THE BEST CAT PUBLICATIONS
MAGAZINES

Cat Fancy (800) 468-1618
Cats (800) 829-9125
Natural Pet (888) 333-0351
Pet Life (800) 767-9377

NEWSLETTERS

Catnip: The most academic of the major newsletters. Put out by Tufts University College of Veterinary Medicine. (800) 829-0926.

CATsumer Report: (800) 968-1738. The most fun newsletter to read; also has special issues analyzing food products, kitty litter, pesticides, etc.

Cornell CatWatch: New but very promising publication from Cornell University College of Veterinary Medicine. (800) 829-8893.

- **Vet Info** is filled with lots of excellent information on cats. Mike Richards, D.V.M., was once the head of AOL's Pet Care Forum and is extraordinarily knowledgeable. This site is head and whiskers above most cat info sites. http://www.vetinfo.com

- **NetPet Central.** Nationwide free posting board for lost, found, or for-sale pets. http://www.keyone.com/pets

- **Pet Channel.** Well-designed resource for cat owners, with editorial material from *Cat Fancy* magazine, *Natural Pet*, and *Pet Products News.* http://www.petchannel.com

- **Today's Pet Online.** Veterinarian Dr. Debbye Turner hosts this interactive Web site developed by *Today's Pet* cable television series. http://www.tviweb.com

- **Healthypet.** The American Animal Hospital Association's Web site gives basic health information as well as a list of animal hospitals they accredit. http://www.healthypet.com

- **rec.pets.cats FAQ Homepage.** Put together by Cindy Tittle Moore from rec.pets.cats, this encyclopedic resource for cat owners and fanciers is a must. http://www.zmall.com/pet/cat-faqs

- **Lightning Strike Pet-Loss Support Page.** We hope you won't have to use this Web site—it's for people who have lost a beloved pet. http://www.netwalk.com

- **The Pet Place,** from the eponymous TV show, has lists of animal shelters, earthquake preparedness tips, etc. http://www.otn.com/ThePetPlace

- **Cats Magazine.** Invaluable information from *Cats* magazine including chat, articles, items to buy, pictures, cartoon caption contest, etc. http://www.catsmag.com

- **Cat Fancy.** Cat chat, photo contests, and more, along with articles from the publication. http://www.catfancy.com

- **Petsmart,** the chain store's pet site has, among other interesting things, pictures of animals you can download for your kids to color. http://www.petsmart.com

- **Steve Dale's pet info.** Several of Steve Dale's witty articles are on this unusual Web site. It's well worth a visit.
  http://www.Chicago.Tribune.com/go/pets

- **NetPets,** containing links to hundres of articles, is a huge resource for all kinds of information on cats.
  http://www.netpets.com

- **Direct Book Service** lets you order any of their 2,000 cat and dog book titles, and read info on the books, authors, etc.
  http://www.dogandcatbooks.com

- **"277 Secrets Your Cat Wants You To Know"** contains ten sections from this book, graciously posted for us by the inimitable Cybergrrl (Aliza Sherman)
  http://www.cybergrrl.com/planet/book/cooper

- **"277 Secrets Your Dog Wants You To Know"** contains "The top 10 Dog Secrets" from our book, "277 Secrets Your Dog Wants You to Know."
  http://www.cybergrrl.com/planet/book/cooper

In our opinion, the three best places to learn about cats on your computer are:

1) **Internet newsgroups such as rec.pets.cats** and **alt.animals.feline** which contain a lot of fascinating tips and information from cat owners.

2) **America Online:** the Pet Care Forum, headed by Dr. Stuart Turner, contains many interesting and informative message groups, such as Dr. Steve Aiken's "Today's Cat Fact" and Gina Spadafori's "Pet Connection."

3) **CompuServe** has two great places for cat information. The "TW Pets Dogs & Cats Forum" (which has Dr. Margaret Muns as staff veterinarian in the dog health, cat health, and cat behavior sections) and "CATS."

THE TOP REASONS CATS DON'T LIKE COMPUTERS

By Paulette Cooper, adapted from a joke about dogs

Cats Don't Like Computers Because...

They can't look out of Windows 95.

The sleep command is not available on all platforms.

It's too difficult for them to "mark" Web sites that they visit.

They can't stop themselves from pouncing on the screen when they hear "You've Got Mail."

They can't smell the catnip icon.

Male cats keep returning to www.pethouse.com instead of working.

They're not fooled by the Kibbles & Bits Screen Saver.

There are no emoticons that look like litter boxes.

After typing for a little while, their Carpal Paw Syndrome starts acting up again.

Their meowing keeps activating the voice recognition software.

SmellU-SmellMe is still in beta phase.

If they can't master SIT and STAY, how are they going to understand advanced commands?

They keep trying to bite the mouse.

They can't find the newsgroup alt.wake.master.up.

They like humping a soft object around the house better than talking dirty in a chat room.

And, finally, the reason some cats *do* like computers: on the Internet, no one knows if they're neutered.

Suggested Reading about Cats

The following books, articles, and newsletters were all sources for this book, and we acknowledge the authors, editors, and publishers for their information.

Barish, Eileen. *Vacationing with Your Pet* (3rd edition). Scottsdale, AZ: Pet-Friendly Publications, 1994–97.

Buckle, Jane. *How to Massage Your Cat.* New York: Howell Book House, Macmillan, 1996.

Davenport, Robert. *Pets' Names of the Rich and Famous.* Los Angeles, CA: General Publishing Group, Inc. 1995.

Eckstein, Warren and Eckstein, Fay. *How to Get Your Cat to Do What You Want.* New York: Fawcett Crest Books, published by Ballantine Books, 1990.

Edney, Andrew and Taylor, David. *101 Essential Tips: Cat Care.* London/New York/Stuttgart: Dorling Kindersley, 1995.

Evans, Rod L. and Berent, Irwin M. *The ABC of Cat Trivia: Hundreds of Curiosities about Our Curious Feline Companions.* New York: Thomas Dunne, St. Martin's Press, 1996.

Fleischer, Leonore. *The Cat's Pajamas: A Charming and Clever Compendium of Feline Trivia.* New York: Harper & Row Publishers, 1982.

Fogle, Bruce, D.V.M. *101 Questions Your Cat Would Ask Its Vet If Your Cat Could Talk.* New York: Carroll & Graf Publishers, Inc., 1993.

Fox, Michael W., Dr. (D.Sc., Ph.D., B.Vet. Med., M.R.C.V.S.) *Supercat: Raising the Perfect Feline Companion.* New York: Howell Book House, Macmillan Publishing Company, 1990.

Fox, Michael W., Dr. *The New Animal Doctor's Answer Book.* New York: Newmarket Press, 1984 and 1989.

Haggerty, Arthur J. *How to Get Your Pet into Show Business.* New York: Howell, 1978.

Heim, Judy. *Internet for Cats: A Guide to How You and Your Cat Can Prowl the Information Highway Together.* Daly City, CA: No Starch Press, 1996.

Holland, Barbara. *Secrets of the Cat: Its Lore, Legend and Lives.* New York: Ivy Books, 1988.

Janik, Carolyn and Rejnis, Ruth. *The Complete Idiot's Guide to Living With a Cat.* New York: Alpha Books, A Simon & Schuster Macmillan Company, 1996.

Kunkel, Paul. *How to Toilet-Train Your Cat: 21 days to a Litter-Free Home.* New York: Workman Publishing, 1991.

MacDonald, Mardie. *The Cat Psychologist: Understanding Your Cat.* New York: Perigree Books, published by the Putnam Publishing Group. 1991.

Malone, John. *The 125 Most Asked Questions About Cats (and the Answers).* New York: William Morrow & Company, Inc., 1992.

Morris, Desmond. *Catlore: More About Cats from the Author of Catwatching.* New York: Crown Publishers, Inc., 1987.

Morris, Desmond. *Catwatching: Why Cats Purr and Everything Else You Ever Wanted to Know.* New York: Crown Publishers, Inc., 1986.

Muller, Ulrike. *The New Cat Handbook.* Hauppauge, New York: Barron's Educational Series, Inc., 1984.

Neville, Peter. *Do Cats Need Shrinks: Cat Behavior Explained.* Chicago: Contemporary Books, 1990.

Neville, Peter. *Pet Sex: The Rude Facts of Life for the Family Dog, Cat, and Rabbit.* London: Sedgwick & Jackson Limited, a division of Pan Macmillan Publishers Limited, 1993.

Pitcairn, Richard H. *Dr. Pitcairn's Complete Guide to Natural Health for Dogs and Cats.* Emmaus, Pennsylvania: Rodale Press, 1995.

Reed, John Avalon. *The Whole Kitty Catalog: More Than 800 Terrific Toys, Treats & True Cat Facts for You & Your Kitty!* New York: Crown Trade Paperbacks, 1996.

Rhea, Alice. *Good Cats, Bad Habits: The Complete A-to-Z Guide for When Your Cat Misbehaves.* New York: Fireside Books, published by Simon & Schuster, 1995.

Schneck, Marcus and Caravan, Jill. *Cat Facts: Do Cats Think? Can They Talk? Why are Cats Athletes? An All Color Guide to the World's Best Loved Cat Breeds.* New York: Barnes & Noble, Inc., 1993.

Siegal, Mordecai. *The Cornell Book of Cats: A Comprehensive and Authoritative Medical Reference for Every Cat and Kitten.* Second Edition. Completely Updated and Revised. Edited by Mordecai Siegal. Villard Books, May 1997.

Siegal, Mordecai. *Understanding the Cat You Love: A Guide to Preventing and Solving Behavior Problems in Your Cat.* New York: Berkley, 1994.

Smith, Carin A., D.V.M. *1001 Training Tips for Your Cat: Learning the Expert's Way to a Happy, Loving Purr-Fect Pet.* New York: Dell Publishing, a division of Bantam Doubleday Dell Publishing Group, Inc., 1994.

Vine, Louis L., D.V.M. *Common Sense Book of Complete Cat Care.* New York: Quill, William Morrow, 1978.

Wilbourn, Carole C., *Cats on the Couch.* New York: Macmillan Publishing Co., Inc. 1982.

Wright, John C. with Lashnits, Judi Wright. *Is Your Cat Crazy? Solutions from the Casebook of a Cat Therapist.* New York: Macmillan, A Simon & Schuster Macmillan Company, 1994.

33. A Few Final Things

The 8 Best Ways to Help Cats

- Learn how much of your donation to cat charities goes to CEOs rather than to cats. The brochure *Who Gets the Money* costs $3 plus postage, and is available from Animal People, Box 205, Shushan, NY 12873, or call 360-579-2505.

- Get involved with cat-assisted therapy with the Delta Society's Pet Partner program at 206-226-7357. See if your cat qualifies to visit hospitals, nursing homes, rehab centers, and schools.

- In Australia, there are people killing cats with clubs and pouring gasoline on them and setting them on fire. Write the Australian Embassy at 1601 Massachusetts Avenue, Washington, DC 20036 and encourage them to solve their feral cat problem with a mass neutering program.

- Help the cat population by spaying yours and persuading friends to have their pets altered, too. Remember that 70,000 dogs and cats are born every day because of uncontrolled breeding.

- Report cruelty to local authorities.

- As many as 75 percent of all cats entering shelters are killed. If you want a new cat or kitten, isn't it better to save one of these than to let your cat bring more into the world?

- If you get a coupon for free cat food, take it and donate it to a local shelter or animal adoption place.

- Try to stop local shelters from using decompression chambers to euthanize cats. It's a painful way to die.

Here's What's in "277 Secrets Your Dog Wants You to Know" by Paulette Cooper and Paul Noble, Ten Speed Press.

DO YOU HAVE A DOG—OR A FRIEND WITH ONE?

Here are some of the fun and fascinating secrets found in *277 Secrets Your Dog Wants You to Know: A Doggie Bag of Unusual and Useful Information,* also by Paulette Cooper and Paul Noble and published by Ten Speed Press.

• Is it safe to let your dog kiss you? • What do dogs think about? • Do dogs get VD? • Embarrassing habits of your dog you've been ashamed to ask anyone about • 6 diseases you can give your dog (and 60 he can give you) • Can your dog see TV? • 9 "people foods" never to feed your dog • Does your dog need Prozac? • Is alcohol or marijuana safe for your dog? • The O. J. Simpson case: What the Akita knows • The 5 most difficult dogs to own • Should you vacuum your dog? • Do rawhide chews work? • Does your smoking hurt your dog? • Stopping your dog's fear of thunder • Save your dog with the Heimlich maneuver • New pills that stop your older dog from acting it • Are dogs psychic? • Do dogs go to heaven when they die? • 19 products that could save your dog's life • Nonshock gadget stops dogs from barking • 90 little-known dangers that could kill your dog • Publications that may print photos of your dog • How to stop a dog from biting you or your child • The most expensive gifts to give your dog • How to give him pills or brush his teeth • Do electronic flea collars work? • Scary new way to steal your dog • Dogs need sunscreen too

And much, much more.

Additional Acknowledgments

Most acknowledgments are in the body of the text, but here are a few extra sources. For full citations, see Suggested Reading About Cats (page 229), Cats on the Web (page 225), or The Best Cat Publications (page 225).

Nobody Ever Tells You These Things: Catnip/*CATsumer Report*/Evans and Berendt/Malone/Morris's *Catwatching*/Reed/Vine

Embarrassing Habits of Your Cat You've Been Ashamed to Ask Anyone About: AOL/*Cats* Magazine/Eckstein/Evans and Berendt/Janik and Rejnis/Malone/rec.pets.cats/Rhea/Smith

Getting Your Cat to Love Your More: AOL/CompuServe/Fox's *The New Animal Doctor's Answer Book*/Fox's *Supercats*/Morris's *Cat Watching*/Smith/Elizabeth Marshall Thomas

Stopping Your Cat From Attacking You: CompuServe/Eckstein/Fox/Janik and Rejnis/Neville

Strange Behavior of Your Cat—and How Experts and Cat Owners Explain and Solve Them: AOL/Eckstein/Rhea

Litter Box Blues and Why Your Cat Won't Use It: AOL/*CATsumer Report*/Eckstein/Janik and Rejnis/Malone/rec.pets.cats

Disciplining Your Cat (You Gotta Do It Sometimes): Fox

Getting Your Cat to Stop Waking You Up, Scratching the Furniture, and Other Hard-to-Handle Problems: AOL/ Eckstein/Edney and Taylor/Janik and Rejnis

Saving Money on Cat Items (or Lowering the Tab on Tabby): *CATsumer Report*/CompuServe/rec.pets.cats

Food and Your Cat: AOL/Catnip/*CATsumer Report*/Edney and Taylor/Janik and Rejnis/Malone/Morris's *Catwatching*/Reed

Food Problems—and Is Your Tabby Too Tubby?: *Animal Health Newsletter*/*Cats* magazine/Fogle/Rhea

What You Should (But Probably Don't) Know About Cat Food Cans and Labels: Smith

How to Make Fleas Flee: AOL/Roger Caras/*Pet Dealer*/Dr. Bonnie Wilcox

How to Talk to Your Cat—and Vice Versa: Janik and Rejnis/Smith

Your Cat's World—and Can She See It on TV?: Animal Health Newsletter/AOL/Janik and Rejnis/Malone/Schneck and Caravan

If You're Allergic to Cats, or Have Multiple Cats: Capuzzo/ Fleischer/Fox/Rhea/Smith

Diseases You Can—and Can't—Catch From Your Cat: Animal Health Newsletter/AOL

How to Help Your Cat Live Longer: CompuServe/rec.pets.cats

How to Save Your Cat's Life…: AOL/CATsumer Report/CompuServe/Eckstein/Janik andRejnis/ Rhea/Wilbourn

These Are Dirty Jobs But You've Gotta Do Them: Cats magazine/CompuServe/Dr. Pitcairn's *Complete Guide to Natural Health for Dogs and Cats*/Janik and Rejnis

Losing Your Cat—and Finding Her Again: AOL/Frank Fanning post on CompuServe/Reed

Fascinating Facts About Felines: AOL/Evans and Berendt/ Fleischer/Fogle/Janik and Rejnis/Morris's *Catwatching*/Reed/ Schneck and Caravan

How Smart Is Your Cat…: CompuServe

Traveling and Holiday Hell: Janik and Rejnis/Wilbourn

Taking Photos of Your Cat—and Getting Them Printed in Magazines and Newspapers: CompuServe

Legal, Landlord, and Pet Insurance Questions: Anmarie Barrie's *Dogs and the Law*/Mary Randolph's *Dog Law*

New Age Cats: Catnip

WHILE YOU WERE READING THIS BOOK…

As many as four thousand cats may have been put to sleep in America in shelters throughout the United States because no one wanted them, or could take them, or there wasn't enough money for the shelters to care for them.

Many of those cats once lived in a house and were someone's adored pet—just like yours.

Quiz for Cat Nuts Only

If you are a genuine cat nut, you are eligible to help us with a survey. You do not have to print your name. Use additional paper if you need it.

We regret that we will be unable to acknowledge or respond to your letters. Please send responses electronically to us at IMOKAYTOO@aol.com or to Paul and Paulette, P.O. Box 20541, Cherokee Station, NY, NY 10021.

1. Do you think your cat is better looking than your spouse or significant other?

2. Do you think your cat has a better disposition than your spouse or significant other?

3. Would you rather cuddle your cat than your spouse or significant other?

4. Do you like your cat better than at least one of your children?

5. Do you trust your cat or your co-workers more?

6. Do you believe your cat will go to heaven one day?

7. If your cat died, would you give up everything you own to bring him back?

8. Do you believe your cat is psychic?

9. Would you risk your life to save your cat's?

10. If you have an opposite-sex cat, have you ever been embarrassed getting dressed in front of him or her?

11. If your cat could save the life of one hundred people you didn't know, but he would have to die now to do it, what would you do?

12. If your cat was dying, and the treatment would cost you every cent you have, would you go for it?

13. If you could live in much better housing for the same amount of money but it meant giving up your cat, would you?

Index